G000017991

london
walking

a handbook for survival
simon pope
illustrations by claudia schenk

●●●ellipsis

first published 2000 by ●●●ellipsis / www.ellipsis.com / text © 2000 simon pope / illustrations © 2000 claudia schenk / british library cataloguing in publication / a cip record for this book is available from the british library / isbn 1 84166 056 6 / printed in hong kong ●●●ellipsis is a registered trademark of ELLIPSIS LONDON LTD / 2 rufus street / london n1 6pe / for a copy of the ellipsis catalogue or information on special quantity orders of ellipsis books please contact the sales department (020 7739 3157 or sales@ellipsis.co.uk)

contents

introduction   11

starting / walk to the shops / carry-out / walk to the cashpoint
walk to the bus or tube / early morning travel / parfum d'homme
walk to your car / walk in your flat   13

defining / defining london / boundaries and limits / grafitti
street names / unnamed byways   22

navigating / methods / improvised navigation / handspan
armspan / moon and stars / tall buildings as landmarks / true
and magnetic north / directional walking / follow the van / not
knowing the exit / lichen and fungi / walking and changing
signs of change / regeneration / also known as / film and
television crews / the pavement / fancy cake or coffee shops
the gutter / signage / street lighting / changing boroughs:
shoreditch and southwark / recording change / lists   25

structuring / integral city / the new mayor / visual alignment
isolated state / social city / cellular city / cellular phones / at
the edge / blackbird and robin / looking for walford / costermongers and the monarchs of walford / some techniques for
reconstructing walford / restrictive architectural elements
walking inside buildings / lobby dangers / physical barriers

roadside barriers and fencing / temporary barriers at roadworks
security fences and barriers / steel wires / bollards / bollard
manoeuvres / d.i.y. stile / other ways over   44

linking / the straight track / building ley lines / consumer geomancy
dowsing / desire lines / implemented / unimplemented   64

open spaces and common land / rights to roam / enclosure
common ownership / finding common land / notable exceptions
royal parks / hampton court palace / fractal lawns / slow walks
ambling / mooching / stroll / the ox walk meanders / ancient
rights of way / ways into the city of london by foot / vantage
points / vantage points architectural / hidden river beds / a
short section of the tyburn river / london's other rivers   72

symbols and way markers / useful implements for making
temporary signage   88

walk from east to west, from sunrise to sunset / hours of
darkness one instance of the east–west walk / south bromley /
poplar limehouse / ratcliff and stepney / whitechapel / janet
cardiff: the missing voice (case study b) / the city / holborn /
covent garden / soho / marylebone / tyburn and paddington /
bayswater notting hill / north kensington / east acton and the
beginnings of suburbia / the end: west acton / ealing and
beyond   90

road traffic / what is traffic? / the rule of the road / types of
driver / maybe it's because / when to give way / the highway
code   119

crossing / crossing the road / where to cross / official recommendation / beware the white van bearing gifts / find a safe place / street games / the six types of crossing situation / the golden rules for using a zebra crossing / being visible / reflective clothing / be decisive / how to cross / do as i say: kerb drill tufty club   124

the kerb / kerb construction / kerb profiles / the limits of the kerb / holding hands / platooning / crossing velocity walking speeds / traffic control symbols / other pedestrian crossing systems / the barnes dance / the footbridge / a law unto yourself / jaywalking / dangerous but effective traffic speed calculator / fender dodging / know the flow soho flow   139

rush hours / personal space / use of mobile (cellular) phones in contraflow / chest and shoulder blocking / the rush hour as machine for memory   156

the underpass / walking in underpasses / marble arch / the marble arch labyrinth / light and dark / glare / typical light levels   158

crossing the river / why cross the river? / north vs south / the thames / official river walks / bridges / pedestrian access official use / things to do on London's bridges / look at the view the bridges at night / flow of workers on bridges / useful techniques for city bridges / walking with the flow / umbrellas bag / danger of theft / shoes / suits / hair / walking against the flow / a note to visitors   162

up and down / escalators / travolators / simple rules for using travolators / the outside / spiral stairways / descending the

staircase / spiral stair techniques / stairs: look for the signs
steps and geography / pavements and surfaces / anatomy of a
typical pavement / paving materials / flags and slabs surface
detail and footwear / same place, different shoes / high heels /
high heel technique / who to buy   172

surviving weather conditions / hot weather / overheating
weight of clothing / blast of a/c / cool shower / cold weather
wind chill / formula for calculating wind chill / walking in cold
weather / warmth for free / hotspots / coldspots / the urban
heat island / wet / puddles / the danger of other people's
umbrellas / undercover in oxford street / observations on in-
store shortcutting / shadow walk   185

timing / human metabolism / body's demands / knowing when to
eat / low blood sugar / burn calories like crazy / calorific values
of specific cakes and pastries / favourite cake and pastry
outlets / the business of walking / people / nautical timepieces
time and space / time and product / receipts / moving / number
of walkers / following / double or quits / what's the time mr wolf
stalker / group walking issues / speed of movement / walkers,
wanderers, night walkers, loiterers / taxi crawl / identifying the
minicab / on being solicited by minicabs / chronometers / public
timepieces / other people's watches / by request / by stealth
public clocks / half-finished public chronometric devices
sundials   197

fitness / breathing / pollutants / how to avoid intake of
pollutants / use side streets / wear a mask / check air pollution
stats / illness / walk to escape the plague / injury / ankle injury
/ shin splints / prevention of injury / blisters / shoes for
diabetics / blood   219

clothing / looking good / trainers / shit on your shoes / hats
warning to hat wearers / feeling good / footwear overhaul
footbath / smell / toilets / entrapment of trespassers   227

paper random-walk generator   235
walk this way   240
bridge typology   244
site notes   251
select bibliography   254

(Throughout the text, map coordinates given are from the standard edition of the *A–Z London Street Atlas*.)

For Fred, Crete and Ronnie Angel: walkers old and new

introduction

I don't envy the rich
In their automobiles.
'Cos the motor car is phoney
I'd rather have shanks' pony.
Strollin' (Reader)

London Walking is a handbook for survival. It explores the city from ground level, relates it to lived experience, and is both a practical guide and a spur for dreams and new possibilities. It hinges on local knowledge and street-smarts which span such subjects as crossing the road, playing street games and 'how to build your own portable stile'. Even techniques learned in rural and suburban climes become invaluable when applied in an urban context. How far can you walk in a day, following the sun?

London Walking explores the many liminal zones where the city contests its existence: at the borders with its suburbs, in districts defined by residents rather than by property developers. It engages with the continual slippage of rich into poor, natural resource into capital, leisure into work and all the things in between that make Westminster and the City of London metropolitan rather than merely urban.

While the book offers plenty of practical advice, it also contains a personal commentary. The book is written both 'on' the subject' and 'through' it; hard fact culled from academic research and government reports lies beside texts which are unknowing and exploratory; descriptions of both new places found by chance and familiar ones are modified in the light of newly-applied technique.

starting

To anyone but the walker London can seem hostile and fragmented, everything an imposition; its inhabitants scared,
insipid, lonely, too cowardly to speak or to make eye-contact as they hide inside 300-odd pages of no-talent novelists,
from home to work and back again.

Walk London and you get to understand the intercon-
nectedness of its districts. Your movement less restricted, the
zones that appear strictly demarcated by money, blood or
tradition soon open to your interpretation.

If you are new to walking, begin with the familiar. Make
short but useful trips, with clear goals and ways to measure
achievement. Use walking instrumentally; in this way, it will
no longer feel like an anomaly in your life.

walk to the shops

Most good shopping involves walking at some point, either
as a means of arriving at the shops or as a way of browsing
the goods on offer.

There is no snobbery in the ground-level activities that
constitute shopping; it is the great leveller, without prejudice
or front. It is walking that performs this function most tan-
gibly: the commingling of classes, of culture and wealth in
the face of consumer products sums up far better the shopping experience than does the moment of purchase, when

dreams are shattered by the crushing weight of credit, debit and debt.

Far less successful is 'personal shopping', where rich or celebrity consumers experience an ersatz retail environment, hugged by a sofa in the top-floor back-room of some department store. This robs us all of the moment of frisson when the ultra-rich and ultra-poor potentially inhabit the same physical and psychological space for a brief moment, cutting through the fug of class hatred that typifies a good day out anywhere in Britain.

CARRY-OUT Purchase made, a pedestrian confronts an immediate problem: how to carry the goods home. A common mistake is to over-shop, typically at a supermarket, and to be overladen with goods. There are several solutions on offer here:

1 Purchase less. When shopping, use a handheld basket to gauge the weight of your potential purchases. When your arm aches, you are at the limit of your ability to carry goods.
2 Employ a device to help spread the load. Use a broom handle or similar, rested across your shoulders from which to hang bags of shopping.
3 Use an improvised 'palm and finger protector' to enable you to carry more supermarket-style polythene carrier bags. A short stick laced through the handles can be held, rather than gripping the ever-thinning polythene handles themselves. A development of this device, a protective sleeve, can be threaded over the handles of a bag to give a larger surface area on which to grip.

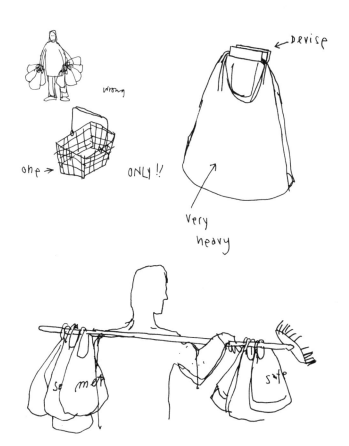

wrong

one → ONLY !!

devise

very heavy

so meh

style

walk to the cashpoint

If you have a bank or building-society account, you may have a card that enables you to withdraw notes from a 'cashpoint', 'hole in the wall' or ATM. Although London's streets are lined with banks and building societies, be cautious about withdrawing money from a bank to which you do not belong, as you may incur a service charge; just another way to discourage the use of hard cash for retail transactions.

1   Identify the cashpoint that belongs to your bank of choice.
2   Appear to walk past the cashpoint, Give nothing away. Let no one second-guess you.
3   Turn as late as possible, giving no warning to other pedestrians.
4   Give no indication as to location of wallet or purse.
5   Take care not to cut-in on other walkers
6   Stand away from queue when waiting your turn. This advice runs contrary to that for other, less urban parts of Britain, where personal safety is taken for granted and such a technique would leave you wide open to the queue jumper.
7   Beware of those who enter into close proximity with you at or near the cashpoint. It has been known for thieves to mark their victim at this juncture, striking once they have moved well away from the scene, even once they are aboard public transport some time later.
8   Shield number with body.
9   Turn sideways, then in the opposite direction. This gives you full view to both left and right. As good as having eyes in the back of your head and it alerts potential

hole in the wall

pretend to walk past,
then do a sharp
u-turn.

pretend not to queue

hell

assailants to your readiness for battle.
10 Use peripheral vision.
11 'Remove cash promptly'.
12 Move back to mid-pavement as soon as is practical.

walk to the bus or tube

Londoners who commute from home to work will have a preferred mode of public transport. As a rule of thumb, those in the north will be happy to use the many local tube stations and new, electronically tagged and regulated buses. Those in the south will have access to a sporadic service of old buses and geographically remote tube stations and will still be happy to use them. Despite these discrepancies, many Londoners nonetheless choose to travel for around two hours daily as they make their way to and from work. They know timetables by heart, heat up when a vehicle is late, cool off when they manage to get a seat. The walk to the bus or tube will be made unconsciously, an habitual movement, almost by instinct, and always, always along the same route. This walk is often considered an inconvenience rather than an asset, a monotonous chore to be inwardly resented.

Commuters can use this enforced period of walking to explore alternative routes to their destination, perhaps using a map to begin with, then taking the bold step of walking unaided through unfamiliar streets. This will, however, break the routine which generally binds commuters' lives together and should therefore be entered into with caution. Weekends or holidays may be used to rehearse other routes free from the pressure of time.

EARLY MORNING TRAVEL

It may come as a shock to visitors who travel during morning rush hour to see the physical state of the capital's young and restless. Far from being the slick, hyper-styled, warm-glowing *über*-youth as relayed in adverts, the crush of bodies at this time in the morning is ugly: unmade-up or with lipstick applied as scrawl before the insertion of contact lenses, hair still wet from the last-minute shower, shirts corrupted by double creases down the sleeve. The sartorial state of Britain should not be judged by London's standards.

PARFUM D'HOMME

Young male London likes to over-adorn itself with gentlemen's aftershave products. Never breath deeply when walking during early evening in densely populated areas, as the air-born perfume can play havoc with respiration. Walk through Selfridges men's grooming department or casually flick through men's style magazines to check which brands will be hitting the streets in number. Look for those most prominently displayed; advertising might reigns supreme here, winning out over editorial column inches and common sense as this season the zing of citrus is giving way to hints of musk. So popular has cologne become in London that a recent concoction was named after one of the city's most enduring characteristics: 'Have you tried "Contradiction", Sir?'

walk to your car

Car ownership in London is low compared to the rest of the country. Adequate compensation is given, however, by the capital's fine public-transport network. For those who still drive in the city, the short journey to and from your vehicle presents an easy and accessible entry into the world of walking. No doubt you will have aimed to park your car as near to your residence as possible. As you become more competent at walking and wish to try out some of the more advanced techniques demonstrated in this manual, you can park at increasing distances from home to extend walking time and distance. Set some simple rules to moderate your behaviour. For example, rely a little on chance and end your journey home one minute earlier each day. With luck, you will have left your car at work within the month.

walk in your flat

London's inhabitants currently pay on average £0.09 per square foot per day in rent, compared to the average £0.03 that tenants cough-up elsewhere in Britain. At this rate, it makes sense to get as much from your hired floor area as possible. Once reserved for Rogation Day only, 'beating the bounds' can be made a daily practice by walking around the internal perimeter of your apartment.

Traditionally, this act would have been accompanied by a 'severe thrashing' to reinforce a sense of belonging and responsibility in the participant. Even without such barbarity, the least ambitious walker can still find the motivation to cover most of their floorspace at least once a day given a little focus and direction.

walk your flat

defining

For those of you who pass it without entering, the city is one thing; it is another for those who are trapped by it and never leave. There is a city where you arrive for the first time; and there is another city which you leave never to return. Each deserves a different name …

   Italo Calvino, *Invisible Cities*, 1972

defining london

In the excellent *A Guide to the Structure of London*, Maurice Ash writing in 1972 notes a depopulation of inner London, and a quest for space that pushes the boundaries of the city beyond even the green belt, redefining it, not as a perimeter, but as a green space within a broader metropolitan London. London once had its regions; now it subsumes those regions into its suburbs, as part of itself.

   But there is a palpable difference between these parts that will be discerned at ground level as you walk.

boundaries and limits

London's entire surface area is 390,000 acres; a daunting amount of ground to cover on foot. However, this is nothing in comparison to its 'ecological footprint' as defined in *Creating a Sustainable London* and using the formula of Canadian economist William Rees.

   The following table, drawn from Herbert Girardet's work of 1995 and 1996 illustrates the full impact of London on surrounding land:[1]

Farmland used @ 3 acres/person: 21,000,000 acres
Forest area required by London for wood products @ 0.27 acres/person: 1,900,000 acres

Land area required for carbon absorption (equal to
acreage required for fuel production and biomass) @ 3.7
acres/person: 26,000,000 acres
Total London ecological footprint = 125 times London's
surface area: 48,900,000 acres
Britain's total surface area: 60,000,000 acres

London's boundaries would extend to cover nearly 81.5%
of the total acreage of the UK. If we were to walk the length
or width of London defined in this way, we would end up in
Newcastle or Plymouth, Holyhead or Kendal.

BRIDGES AND BOUNDARIES Where boroughs are separated by
the Thames, maps show their boundaries as running
through the middle of the river itself. When walking, however, you will notice that the south sides of bridges are
claimed for the north. London Bridge has its gun-metal
gryphon at the south side, echoing the old London Bridge
[D1 78] which positioned its Traitors' Gate and drawbridge
in a similar location. Blackfriars [A7 62] is annexed in a
comparable fashion.

GRAFFITI The limits of inner London can be gauged by mea-
suring the form and quantity of extreme nationalist graffiti.[2]
At the very edges of inner London more recent and topical
slogans are scrawled for the walker to read; they usually
appear on street furniture such as phone junction boxes or
the handrails of footbridges. Sometimes a trail of stickers
may be set, typically posted by hetero-sceptic 'third position'
Ruralists, engaged in a 'life and death struggle for England's
existence', at the margins in East Acton.

More graphically simplistic graffiti such as the National

Front's NF symbol can be seen within inner London. There is, however, comparatively little in the way of current extreme nationalist graphical propaganda in the central districts of London.

street names

According to the Central Intelligence Agency's *World Factbook* there are no 'unpaved' highways in the UK. All roads of note receive a 'functional classification': M, A, or B. Still, much walking can be done on the undocumented surfaces overlooked by international security forces on roadways known by name rather than number.

UNNAMED BYWAYS You may also walk along unnamed or misnamed walkways, places which are in constant use by local people who are free to change names according to use, personal experience or local dialect. Some places even remain unnamed.

Borough Market [DI 78], for example, has several unnamed byways. Some have been given informal names – such as 'The Back Passage', after the private practices of a much-hated local dignitary, and 'Twat Alley' after the recently famous and excessively lifestyled young television chef who used it as a location in his second Essexploitation series for the BBC.

navigating

There is a margin of error inherent in every form of navigation due to the limits of the methods themselves; some will make personal error more likely than others. It is useful to be able to call upon a range of navigation techniques to be deployed in a given situation.

methods
You may wish to use traditional scientific devices such as maps or a compass to help you walk around the city, or you may prefer to use less exact means.

IMPROVISED NAVIGATION Studies have shown that there are three ways in which we orientate ourselves: through the use of landmarks; route knowledge; and 'overview' maps in which we piece together known routes to build a mental model of a terrain.

Stranded without an *A–Z*, it is this local knowledge that counts, but as a visitor or disoriented inhabitant, you cannot count on such local street-smarts. You will have to use whatever is immediately available. The following techniques may help:

HANDSPAN Most people will have a handspan of about 20 degrees. People with small hands may have a handspan of

① orientation
② smell
③ sound
④ horizon

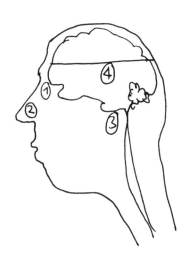

15 degrees or so, while people with big hands may be able to stretch to 25 degrees.

> ARMSPAN Stand with arms outstretched to each side along the baseline. If the baseline is a fence or wall, lean against the structure and settle into a position where pressure from the structure is the same on both sides of the body. Now bring both hands together with the arms outstretched. The line from your nose, to the join between the hands when the finger tips are level should be at 90 degrees to the baseline.
> *The Bushwalkers' Guide to the Galaxy*[3]

MOON AND STARS Remember to take the movement of the moon and stars across the night sky into consideration. Use them only as rough landmarks. The moon rises in the east and sets in the west, so observing it for a short while will give you some added directional reference.

Generally, the orange glow from the city's streetlights will obscure all but the brightest stars.

TALL BUILDINGS AS LANDMARKS Unlike celestial bodies, London's tallest buildings provide a fixed geographical reference point:

1 Chicago had its 'Ferris Wheel' in 1893. London had its 'London Eye' [K2 77] in 2000. Walking towards British Airways' giant rotating monument to the millennium will take you to Jubilee Gardens on the South Bank. Marvel at its mock 'industrial age' spoked splendour.
2 Following the flashing light on top of Canary Wharf [D1 80] will take you towards Docklands and the north end of the Isle of Dogs.

3 Centre Point [H6 61] has its name emblazoned on its upper floors and it stands at St Giles Circus, the less glamorous end of Oxford Street.

true and magnetic north

True North is geographic north or the direction to the North Pole. A compass will point to magnetic north when there are no influences from the local environment. Metropolitan London is not a mining region, so there is little influence from the soil, but some steel footbridges send compasses into a frenzy.

directional walking

> Eastward I go only by force; but westward I go free.
> Henry David Thoreau, 'Walking'

Thoreau preferred to walk west. It is one of life's conundrums that wherever you live, the rich always live in the west. Dr Pevsner alludes to this (MacInnes, 1966: p126) when noting that George Peabody's statue at the Royal Exchange [D6 62] faces west, away from the poor whom he helped to rehouse. Always having a nose for money, George now faces north, an indication that big money is on the move, sizing up the King's Cross slum-clearance schemes.

RECORDING THE DIRECTION IN WHICH YOU WALK

1 With the aid of a map, record the location of your starting point.
2 Walk towards your destination point.
3 Take a compass.
4 Record the location of your final destination.
5 Calculate the direction of your walk using the compass and map.
6 Plot the direction of your walks on a simple graph with 'days' or

$15° - 20°$

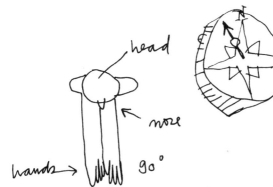

head

nose

hands

$90°$

'number of journey' on the x axis, and 'direction' on the y axis. Direction could be expressed as either degrees or cardinal points. Look for a 'flat-line' which will indicate a high frequency of uni-directional walking. Over time, patterns will emerge. There may be some days on which you regularly walk in an atypical direction.

follow the van

Miss Marie Lloyd, 'Our Marie', once exhorted us not to 'dilly dally on the way' when following the van. With our old cock linnet and all the contents of our home in transit, this exercise was once popular among rent-dodgers throughout the city. Removal vans of this type are now few and far between. Waiting for one to come along in order to follow it and give structure to your walk would take immense patience and an amount of time that few can spare in today's economic climate.

Other types of vans are more commonly found on the streets of London. In some areas you will be able to follow them for an extended period of time, since dense traffic reduces their pace to that of a pedestrian. Try following some of these:

ICE CREAM VAN walk and maintain a high calorie-intake.

POLICE 'RIOT' VAN walk with an audience of six.

TRANSIT 'RENTAL' VAN always white. Easy to lose track of.

DELIVERY VAN UPS's brown and tan livery is easy to spot in a crowd.

AA OR RAC VAN more highly conspicuous liveries.

POST OFFICE VAN they always follow the same route and travel at approximately the same time every day. Very useful for generating a regular schedule of walking.

THE HARD LIFE: 'My Old Man Said, "Follow the Van"', sung by Miss Marie Lloyd, written by Charles Collins and Fred W Leigh:

We had to move away, 'cos the rent we couldn't pay,
The moving van came round just after dark;
There was me and my old man, shoving things inside the van,
Which we'd often done before let me remark.
We packed all that could be packed in the van and that's a fact;
And we got inside all we could get inside,
Then we packed all we could pack on the tailboard at the back,
Till there wasn't any room for me to ride.

Chorus: My old man said, 'Follow the van, don't dilly dally on the
    way!'
Off went the cart with the home packed in it,
I walked behind with me old cock linnet.
But I dillied and dallied, dallied and dillied,
Lost the van and don't know where to roam.
Variation: I stopped on the way to have the old half-quartern,
And I can't find my way home.

I gave a helping hand with the marble wash-handstand,
And straight, we wasn't getting on so bad;
All at once the carman bloke had an accident and broke,
Well, the nicest bit of china that we had.
You'll understand of course, I was cross about the loss,
Same as any other human woman would;
But I soon got over that, what with 'two-out' and a chat,
'Cos it's little things like that what does you good.

Chorus
Variation: Now who's going to put up the old iron bedstead
If I can't find my way home?

Oh! I'm in such a mess – I don't know the new address –
Don't even know the blessed neighbourhood,
And I feel as if I might have to stay out all the night,
And that ain't going to do me any good.
I don't make no complaint, but I'm coming over faint,
What I want now is a good substantial feed,
And I sort o' kind o' feel, if I don't soon have a meal,
I shall have to rob the linnet of his seed.

Chorus
Variation: You can't trust the specials like the old-time coppers
When you can't find your way home.[4]

not knowing the exit

There are a minimum of three ways to find the nearest exit
from the platform when aboard a tube train, apparently
without looking:

1 Luck. Turn left or right or straight ahead. There's a one-
in-three chance of heading in the correct direction.
2 Travel the same route every day, stand at the same spot on
the same platform for the last x number of years. The alignment of carriage to exit becomes ingrained. The brain
knows, the body knows, memory etched into tensed arms
and legs, *Standard* under left arm, briefcase in right hand.
People like this are on auto-pilot. Don't look on in awe.
Theirs is a life of little skill or challenge – lab rats with the
clock ticking.

WAY OUT

3 Read the signs. Appear to be a Londoner by 'reading' the station as the train slows to a halt. First, use peripheral vision to check which side of the carriage the platform is on. There's nothing that gives you away more than standing intently at a door, only to find it's on the wall-side of the platform. Once you've clocked it, scan the area above the platform, where the signage indicating which line you are on is located. At regular intervals, a small black sign bearing yellow letters will tell you 'exit', indicating the direction to the nearest exit with an arrow. Keep and eye on these as your train slows to a stop. As you pass an exit, the arrows will change direction.

lichen and fungi as indicator of levels of pavement use

Tests published in the *Scientific Journal of Orienteering* in 1998 showed that even repeated trampling by highly stressed runners failed to destroy any species of moss or fungus growing on the logs underfoot. However, although lichen and fungi thrive in clean air, evidence in West Acton proves that they also thrive where they receive little contact with walkers. The empty pavement of the Christ Army stronghold in Emanuel Avenue [s6 57] is one of the few places in London where such vegetation grows unmolested.

walking and change

Some people think change can be mastered; some think that it can be engineered.

When walking, the change that you'll notice will be that which reveals itself to you at ground level. You'll probably not be privy to the plotting and planning of local government and investors, of the small-time barons' and dictators' A4 laminated photocopies tied to lampposts below eye-level, warning of planning permission applied for, of road closure and blocked pavements. These are indicators of imminent change, interim inconveniences pending the larger structural changes that will come. From these dry descriptions in the arcane dialects of highway regulation, you can't possibly imagine the dramatic shifts in class structure and atmosphere that will affect these streets.

Keep an eye out for the signs of real change: shifts in brand-loyalties, from sweet wrappers to parked cars.

signs of change

Scan the environment at different resolutions to notice different kinds of change. Some reveal themselves at your feet, others are noticeable only from distance and or even only through time.

Here are some resolutions you might choose:

1 pavement level;
2 street level;
3 postal district;
4 council district.

regeneration

Much of inner London has had some form of inward investment in recent years: a 'City Challenge' scheme such as that in Brixton, or the over-extension of an international bank and its workers into such places as Bermondsey and Spitalfields.

ALSO KNOWN AS ... When the demand for an urban dwelling in a 'property hot spot' way outstrips supply there's one sure-fire way for an estate agent to lever more profit from the situation – the expansion of the geographical definition of 'fashionable area'. This is undertaken through linguistic sleight-of-hand, edges of hot zones extended through alchemical processes. Therefore:

Stoke Newington borders = Clapton;
South Dulwich = Nunhead;
Notting Hill = North Kensington;
Shoreditch = South Hackney;
Hoxton = Shoreditch.

As a walker you will be privy to the fretwork of qualitative difference between a district in its stable and excited states.

FILM AND TELEVISION CREWS The presence of film or television crews signals that things are changing. These changes will ultimately be expressed through an increase in property prices.

The media in London enter into a cannibalistic cycle. Film location-finders often initiate the process, selecting a suitably downmarket borough whose council will take lesser amounts of money for the inconvenience of having Sean Connery and supporting cast descend upon them at peak traffic times. On release of the film some one to two years later this will ensure articles in magazines such as *Marie Claire* or *The Guardian*'s 'Space' supplement on Thursdays. These are then seized upon by national television as documentary fodder, which in turn sends local news crews into panic as they realise that they've reneged on the obligations made in their licensing application to the ITC and that they should get to grips with local issues about local people.

THE PAVEMENT The replacement of old composite flagstones and uneven cobblestones with hand-cut Portland stone is a sure sign of regeneration. One example is Cleaver Square [A5 78] in Kennington where Lottery aid was given to renovate the pavement and add high detail, such as keystoned pavement radii and granite curbing. High-specification building development has accelerated noticeably in the area since their introduction.

FANCY CAKE OR COFFEE SHOPS There's a trend for such shops to place their tables and chairs on the pavement in a (usually vain) bid to cultivate what was once called a 'continental' air. As a walker, it can be useful to to get rest and refreshments while still maintaining contact with your familiar roadside territory. Use this time, outside-but-stationary, to reflect on the intellectual practice of *flânerie*. In affluent and regenerative districts you will often see the upper and middle classes indulging themselves in this nineteenth century practice of self-conscious and idle display. The *flâneur* is a vogueish role model for those who use the street as escape rather than through necessity, aping Oscar Wilde's notorious dilettante and class-tourist Dorian Grey.

THE GUTTER Keep your eyes to the floor. Should your district or borough be 'on the up', your gutter will now contain:

- new cars;
- chauffeurs waiting in new cars.

signage

RENAMING OF DISTRICTS This is inevitable once private developers get in on the act. Housing schemes have always pandered to estate agents' need to lie, and their imposition of grandiose monikers. Most common in London, with its many warehouse developments, has been the adoption of the 'wharf' brand, alluding to the triumphant industrial and service sectors of the colonial empire; hence 'Gun Wharf' [B1 64], 'Horseshoe Wharf' [D1 78] (which, incidentally, was to be called 'Shoehorn Wharf'), and 'Butlers' Wharf' [E1 78], named in honour of the many who served so few.

CORPORATE TAGGING One obnoxious addition to Southwark's upwardly destined borough of Borough is the unwanted tagging of streets by private traders. Witness the surge in street signs – small enough to be unobtrusive but also too small to read – around the Stoney, Park and Clink Street area [D1 78]. With arrows pointing to obvious features and street names which duplicate those on standard road signs, these appeared just as an enormous wine warehouse museum opened its doors to the public. This indicates the huge gulf in understanding between those who have lived and worked here and the new business interests which have moved in and who rarely live their lives in the public space of the street. The street signs on London Bridge [D1 78] go over peoples heads, literally – 10-foot-tall poles way out of reach and beyond the inquiring eye. Useless.

Under one arch in Stoney Street near Borough Market you can see the evidence of change written in large white letters. 'Bankside' declaims the 20-foot-high corporate graffito. Not Borough; not Borough Market; not Southwark; not even 'London's Larder', but 'Bankside'. In reality this is a short stretch of walkway between Southwark Bridge and the site of the old Clink prison, an area that epitomises the cultural-property-developer's dream of surmounting the doomed post-war South Bank Centre [K1 77] with a pastiched and reclaimed Little England-on-Thames. Bounded by the Millennium Wheel in the west and London Bridge in the east, the Millennium Walkway takes us through a 'thousand years of adventure'. The showpiece is the 'cathedral of power', the Bankside Tate or Tate Modern [B7 62], housed in a gigantic former power station, putting art and culture into the realm of nationalised industry where coal once reigned.

PUBLIC ART AND CHANGE The Bankside regeneration has been host to several low-key official art interventions. The pavements of Borough High Street were inlaid with new aggregate slabs for example, displaying the name of the current adjacent business premises, forming a hardening or crust at a particular premillennial moment in time; a geological layer left for future generations to speed-read rather than slowly decipher. The only trouble is that many of the shops on the street are known by previous owners' names or none at all: 'the shop that Keogh's used to own', for example, or 'that place where we buy the sandwiches'.

Fixing the names of the members of the local traders' association in stone only speaks to the local authorities. It has little to do with the way that language is used in everyday life. But when you're walking, it cheers you up no end to have the bank under your heel for a change

STREET LIGHTING There's a simple equation: the more evocative an area of London is of Dickensian squalor or the more redolent it is of the Ripper's East End, the more ripe it is for adoption by the gentrifiers. Some areas of London still fail to frustrate such perceptions – images of a dimly lit London

Town, with its fogs; the 'grey flannel mists' of *Dorian Gray*;[5] the 'pea-soupers' of Blitz-era *Picture Post* magazines – but they are now few. Gareth Steadman Jones (Jukes 1990: p17) indicates that the various areas of London to have Dickens' mind 'stamped' on them, such as Saffron Hill and Jacob's Island, underwent the most cruel and vicious redevelopment processes in the middle of the nineteenth century. In some senses this is still the case.

We can maybe widen the scope of literary material which has such an effect on London: Iain Sinclair and Peter Ackroyd in the east, Nick Hornby in the north and, most spectacularly, Richard Curtis in the west.

Once there are smarter cars parked in their streets at night, local authorities ensnare further high-bracket council-tax payers by extending and upgrading the streetlights in the area. This confers a feeling of security and homeliness to such newcomers – invariably affluent, young, single men – whose demographic profile perfectly matches those at highest risk from violent street crime.

Changes in streetlighting can be one of the first legible signs that the authority wants this area to undergo a radical 'change of use'. As a visiting walker you may see the benefit too: you will be able to see the pavement beneath your feet for example.

Spare a thought for those who used to live here and pray that it doesn't happen to you.

CHANGING BOROUGHS: SHOREDITCH AND SOUTHWARK When the Globe theatre opened in 1599 on the south bank of the Thames it brought with it not only much of the creative talent from the Shoreditch theatre district, but also the timbers of The Theatre, 'London's first playhouse' (Weinred and

Hibbert 1995: p885), re-used to build the Globe. The Theatre had thrived among the low-life of 'Sewer Ditch', located as it was beyond the moral and social constraints of the City walls. That was until Southwark and the 'Liberty of the Clink', with its heady mix of high church, bear fighting and working girls upped the stakes and stole its crown.

But just as the Globe was closed by Puritans in 1642, so some of the more interesting creative enterprises have been forced to move away from Southwark in recent times. Winchester Wharf [D1 78], once home to a clutch of early 'new-media' ventures, is closed. The pendulum has now swung back again – some of the new-media entrepreneurs moved north against the flow, back to Shoreditch, to play with the big boys.

recording change

LISTS Lists are invaluable tools for recording change. In Jeannette Jacobson's compelling *Hazard Hunting – Looking for Trouble*, we are implored to 'Do A Better Job With A Checklist'. Far from being a simple exercise, list-making involves selection and editing at every part of the process. According to Jacobson: 'An appropriate checklist provides your focus at the beginning ... and a sense of closure when you finish.'[6]

It is with this uppermost in our minds that we must choose our checklist:

1 Simple Area Inspection Form
   • one column for the location being observed;
   • one column for what was seen;
   • a third column for comments or needed action. Simple forms are often most appealing since they seem easier to

work with ... If you become distracted or interrupted
during the walk-around, which is common, you may
forget what you've observed. Remember, like the hidden
objects in the picture, some hazards are easily
overlooked.

2   Customised Checklist
    It's easy to find a specific safety checklist for a shop,
    yard, office, warehouse, marine terminal, etc. Even
    complicated operations can be categorised on inspection
    forms that make a huge task manageable.
    Once you've analysed your own operation, you'll know
    which checklists will be most useful for you.
    Customised checklists are efficient because they do part
    of the thinking for you – the part that says, 'Now, what
    is it I'm looking for?' When you're finished, you can feel
    more confident that your sleuthing has covered all the
    bases, and you can move on to other important aspects
    of your job.

3   Scoring System
    Many checklists provide a place to record 'Satisfactory',
    'Unsatisfactory', or 'Not Applicable', including room
    for comments or action items ... A more complex
    scoring system is that which can be monitored over
    time. The most favorable surveys would show high
    scores, while the lower scores might be cause for
    probation and more frequent inspections.

Your observations do not have to find their final form in a
list. They can subsequently be interpreted in many ways. An
example of a visual reworking of a found notebook of lists

is Jem Cohen's 1996 video homage to Walter Benjamin, *Lost Book Found*,[7] which projects the precise, time-limited and hungry list-making of a stranger on to the roving, decentred screen of a Manhattan filmmaker-*flâneur*.[8, 9]

structuring

The metropolis is structured in many different ways at any one moment; its many hierarchies interconnecting, linking also to many other networks to form a constantly rolling, shifting, intricate mesh of multiple dimensions. When walking in London it is possible to divine some of the characteristics of these structures as made manifest through, for example, housing density, the quality of paving or degrees of urban regeneration. 'It is through walking that you will compose the city' (De Certeau 1984: p93). Walking to 'weave places together' (ibid.: p97).

integral city

In order to understand London, many have tried to define it by excluding elements that would dull the sharpness of focus or confuse the clear picture of the capital city. To some, London is the hub of the south-east region. According to Ash in *A Guide to the Structure of London*, the 'South East Study' of 1965 considered its region as

> an empty space – a sort of vacuum aimed at restoring the integrity of London as a city in its own right, centrally integrated and bound together by urban motorways that allowed of all the agitation of movement within itself, rather than dispersed beyond it. (Ash 1972: p69)

With the recent imposition of the new mayoral post, we have London again defining itself as an indivisible unit, a 'self-contained city of high urbanity' (Ash 1972) more concerned with its internal workings than external relationships.

THE NEW MAYOR The mayor (Fuller 2000) presides over a city with an antiqued vision of itself; a fiction made real. Antipoetic forces determined that Jeffrey Archer failed in his attempt to embody this in a neat way, reliving in Technicolor the adventures of Dick Whittington, 'folk hero and wealthy merchant' (Wienreb and Hibbert 1995: p178).

The Dick of legend was a poor man who moved to London from the Vale of Leadon (just off junction 3 of the M50) in the late fourteenth century. He first became cook, then Lord Mayor, having hallucinated that the Great Bells of Bow had pleaded with him not to leave town as he sat atop Highgate Hill [E5 28], saying his goodbyes to the fair city that was treating him so badly.

But fact describes a landowner's son turned mercer, who lent money to royalty, was repaid by becoming Lord Mayor and who acted as benefactor to many of London's great social institutions: Bart's hospital, the Guildhall library, Newgate gaol for example.

It all made sense: substitute Gloucestershire for Somerset, Archer's Alembic House [D5 77] for Whittington's Highgate Hill (Sinclair 1997: p165). It's a shame it can never be …

visual alignment
In the slum clearances of the nineteenth century, straight lines were driven through the very poorest districts of central London. These opened and widened through-routes 'for

the general convenience of public interest' and brought improvements to the deteriorating health and moral standards which were supposed to be caused by cramped living conditions. (Jukes 1990: p15).

As is still the case when property developers smell blood or money, thousands were displaced as the capital's great and good conspired to bring their grand architectural plan to fruition. According to Gareth Steadman Jones, (ibid. p16) more than 40,000 were evicted in the demolition carried out in preparation for Farringdon Road [B4–B5 62]. Countless others suffered the same fate as Holborn Viaduct [B6 62], New Oxford Street [H6 61], Victoria Street [G3 77], Commercial Road [G6–K6 63], Cannon Street [C6–D75 62], and Queen Victoria Street [C6–D7 62] were cut through London's poorest districts.

'isolated state'

The Von Thünen model of the 'Isolated State'[10] has its inhabitants acting to 'maximise profits', making it self-sufficient and surrounded by wilderness. It is a positive match with the contemporary Londoner's view of the relation of the metropolis to the suburbs and, indeed, to the rest of the British Isles.

There have been times when pressures of population have forced London to redefine itself. The old London County Council instigated forced migration schemes, striking friendships with outlying towns and cities to take the 'overspill' off its hands. London under this definition would be bounded by Northampton in the north, Southampton in the south, Swindon in the west, Ipswich and Ashford in the east. London would be left smaller, compact, better resolved in some way. But these schemes were still 'classical' solutions

(Ash 1972). The London conurbation was redefined as the 'south east', a place where 'new cities' could be 'opportunistically embedded'. It was a blank canvas to work into, with no thought for the capital's relationship with its neighbours.

'social city'

Some who sought to control 'urban sprawl' looked to Ebenezer Howard's model of the 'social city':[11] 'a nexus of urban development' (ibid.: p71). As each development grows, it should push up against its 'green belt' of 'real' rural land, and leap over it to establish a 'new town', distinct from the first. In his book of 1898, *To-morrow: A Peaceful Path to Real Reform*, Howard describes the growing metropolis encircled by garden cities, each centred on its own 'Central Park' and 'Crystal Palace'. Milton Keynes stands in testament to modern fantasists working in this vein, still awaiting the full impact of suburban rejuvenation as it reaches a crescendo in the mass media.

cellular city

In *Learning Cellular Automata: Modelling Urban Modelling*,[12] Colonna *et al* describe a 'new generation' of urban modelling which uses 'intelligent' simulation. It is an 'attempt to shift from "classic" to "evolutionary" models (as evolutionism appeared to be the symbol of complex systems)' (ibid.).

To build such models and run simulations on them, cities have to be disaggregated so as to make them legible by computer programs. This involves simplification and abstraction, determining arbitrary boundaries within which factors can be quantified. The process is usually undertaken by placing an orthogonal grid over the subject. The choice of this method 'originates from the morphologic structure of the urban texture of ... American cities and from the corresponding shape of the statistical elementary zones' (ibid.).

This pattern does not exist in cities such as London, or indeed any city which was built before the mid nineteenth century. Its governmental regulations do not correspond to this unit of measurement. Walking reveals the accretion of histories and governances: meandering paths, potholes, multiple unco-ordinated road excavations and arcane, inconsistent parking regulations.

CELLULAR PHONES 'The genius of the cellular system is the realisation that a city can be chopped up into small cells', each used to administer the low-frequency telecommunications network. Mobile phone cells are normally thought of as hexagonal and are typically 10 square miles in area.[13] These forms of cellular automata can perhaps help to model the city, as each cell is itself a generator of regulatory data.

It's now common to hear voices in the street – hands-free sets encourage public speech, bringing the private into the public realm. London now sounds like New York City; no longer do its inhabitants have to mutter under their breath. There's now an excuse to open up the internal dialogue to passers-by.

Look for clues in 'open talkers': eyes fixed on the far distance; little eye movement; neck crooked forward, but standing or sitting very upright; inclusion of the word 'mate' as punctuation in every sentence. With experience you will learn how to gauge where they fit on the continuum between 'safe' phone user and 'deranged' casualty of government healthcare policy.

at the edge

Walking the edges of the metropolis there are tangible signs of all these competing definitions. If, for example, you take an east to west/sun-up to sun-down walk (see page 90), it is possible to feel when you are both entering and leaving 'inner London' and when you hit the ill-defined contested margins, the 'Edge Cities' (Garreau 1991) without legal title or municipal regulation, the 'liminal zones' favoured by cultural-studies lecturers.

These are places where no one walks: too far from the centre of the city; too far from the shops; just near enough to the motorways that lead to the golf courses and country clubs. These are places shaped by the car and train, not by the walker. Being on foot in these areas attracts immediate suspicion, the only redeeming factor being that you might be considered a car-thief, scouting for the sore-thumb GTi among the LS, the LSs and the GLs.

It's out here that sharply defined London gets spoiled: it turns 'wide city'. Suburban. Out here's where under-18s have so little to do and so much time to do it in. Some of us, still bitter about the 'casual' youth culture micro-phenomenon of 1983, just can't shake the onset of panic in these areas. You don't need a compass to know which way to go from here.

BLACKBIRD AND ROBIN

Late at night, especially in the more leafy, residential areas of London, you may hear the plaintive tone of the blackbird or robin. Under normal conditions, you would expect them to be in full song at 5.00, but they have been known to start to sing in the very early hours, often as early as 2.00, confused by the orange glow in the sky as to whether it is nature's dawn.

black bird or robin

black

red

now start again

Their song can be used to generate a zoned walk: these birds are aggressively territorial and keep strictly demarcated areas for themselves. Listen to them in the early hours of the day when they might be the only birds singing and you will be able to hear one local bird and, calling in response, one distant bird.

Rules:
1 Find a local bird. Walk towards it, until it sounds louder than any other bird.
2 Listen as it calls. There will be a distant reply from a neighbouring bird of the same species.
3 Walk towards the neighbouring bird and away from the local one.
4 Keep walking until the neighbour becomes the new local bird.
5 Repeat 1.

looking for walford

London is nothing in itself; its identity defined through its relationship to other things: to ideas, objects, people, places. Often it is the work of fiction that comes to define London with most resonance. Of all the great works of fiction that have been produced there is one that shines brighter than all other literary beacons, stronger than all epics of the big screen. *EastEnders* is the naked 100-watt bulb of fictive London, burning fiercely in the empty hallway that is quality television drama.

Its audience sees London through the producer's eye, a cynical populist filter where public spaces are simplified, made fiction; where representation lords it over tactility. Cheeky, pale, desperate, salt-of-the-earth, loyal: those described are simple folk who inhabit the pavements, the pub, the market, the caff, red buses, clubs and restaurants.

of the placenames is:

Albert Square – one instance: E15
Victoria Road – five instances: E4, E11, E13, E17, E18
Bridge Street – no instances. Nearest is the approach to Westminster Bridge, SW1
George Street – one instance: E16
Turpin Road – no instances. Nearest is in Feltham

Plotting these results, it is possible to estimate the position of Walford as being east of Leyton, north of Plaistow, west of Wanstead Flats and south of Woodford.

2 District names
Walford sounds like districts that exist, and verifiably so, in London:
Walworth – SE17
Wanstead – E11
Taking a mid-point on the direct linear route between these districts we can conclude that Walford is located in Bromley-by-Bow, E3.

3 Etymological analysis
While building a complete array from the root 'Wal' is beyond the scope of this publication, it is possible to focus on the form in relation to its use in London.

Perhaps the most meaningful placename that relates to this enquiry is 'Walbrook', a stream that flowed from Finsbury to the Thames. Its route passed just west of Bank and is commemorated in the naming of Walbrook [C7 62], a street nearby in EC4. This was the shallow stream around which Roman Londinium was sited. The Romans used the

Walbrook as their main water supply and erected a temple to the god Mithras on its eastern bank.

The foundations of this temple, 'a satellite development' to a larger temple whose exact site remains contested (Sinclair 1997: p116) have been exposed to the public once more in the vain belief that a revival of this bull-slaying cult will grant the City supremacy over Wall Street.[15]

By the fourteenth century the Walbrook was an open sewer. By the sixteenth century it was completely covered over. Its rowing club now resides in Teddington.

The second element, 'ford' is 'a shallow place where a river or stream may be crossed by wading or in a vehicle' according to the OED.

In their combined form as 'Walford', both elements point us towards 'a shallow place on the Walbrook which may be crossed'. At its widest, the Walbrook was little more than 14 feet wide, so the ancient Walford could have been sited almost anywhere along its length. Presuming that the Roman settlement was built at the lowest fording-point, we can estimate that the fictive Walford is at the very epicentre of the Cockney myth, somewhere near the Temple of Mithras in EC4, almost within earshot of the bells of St Mary-le-Bow in Cheapside [C6 62].

restrictive architectural elements

WALKING INSIDE BUILDINGS Much of your walking life in London will be spent inside, whether on the underground, in places of historical interest, or within the acres of prime office and retail development that now occupy much of inner London.

Office and retail terrain presents the walker with a highly controlled, richly coded environment. Such spaces extend beyond those which house the armies of pen-pushers and phone operators. Their well-being depends on a network of peripheral spaces, antechambers and inner sanctums, public and private spaces:

- the 'Interzone', 'where everything is permitted that is not forbidden' (Sinclair 1997: p101);
- exterior porch and canopy;
- filtering device such as intercom or turnstile (the Liffe building in Bishopsgate, for example);
- doors (swing or revolving, for example);
- lobby;
- reception;
- security-staff office;
- lifts;
- corridor;
- open-plan office;
- glass-walled, open-door office;
- boardroom;
- refreshment area.

LOBBY DANGERS Walking in lobbies often involves dealing with sudden changes in flooring. Should you be wearing high heels, especially those of metal-tip construction, encountering a hard shiny surface such as marble can have disastrous consequences. Wear a rubber tip as a cure-all.

'Segs' or 'Blakeys', the protective metal plates in the leather or rubber heels of flat shoes, present the wearer with a similar risk of slipping as metal hits marble or tile. Carpets in lobbies are equally dangerous; where 'dragging' occurs, a stumble or fall is likely.

physical barriers

FENCES AND BARRIERS Fences and barriers both protect and frustrate, depending on context. There are times when a well-placed fence can save your life, shielding you from oncoming traffic for example.

ROADSIDE BARRIERS AND FENCING Where traffic is fast-moving, Tension Corrugated Beam (TCB) fence is sometimes used. Park Lane, for example, with its many streams of traffic jostling for premium lane-position as they approach Marble Arch and the run north and west, has barriers capable of withstanding high-speed impact and reducing the risk of cross-over accidents. They also frustrate any attempt to cross the road on foot.

TEMPORARY BARRIERS AT ROADWORKS The British Motorcycle Federation's *Briefing on Wire Rope Safety Fence and Other Vehicle Restraints* 1998[16] notes that 'temporary concrete barriers with interlocking sections which bolt together' will give protection from 50 mph collisions: useful should you encounter roadworks which force you on to the highway by way of temporary footpaths.

SECURITY FENCES AND BARRIERS Often used to control the flow of crowds, guiding torrents of people towards football matches or concerts, they serve to reduce eddies and back-wash.

The standard barriers used to control pedestrians are 2.5 metres (just over 8 feet) long and are usually seen with a galvanised finish. Police-issue versions can invariably be seen in number on Horse Guards Road, SW1 [H2 77]. They are easily identifiable through the patterns of denting: the memory of lower body parts impressed into their grilles.

If you have ever been in close contact with the white version, count yourself lucky; they are used to control Very Important Persons, including royalty. And you.

STEEL WIRES Barbed wire is made to various grades: generally of low-carbon-steel wire with a breaking strain of around 604lb per square foot. A higher quality, high-carbon-steel wire will have a breaking strain of 900lb per square foot.

Commercial razor ribbon or helical wire is made from either galvanised high-tensile steel or stainless-steel wire, with each barb being '2.4 inches +/- 5% long from tip to tip', according to the Alamo Fence Company.[17]

BOLLARDS In technical parlance, bollards 'provide for the separation of pedestrian and vehicular traffic'[18] and are, as such, a useful and necessary addition to the walker's armoury. Within the genus of street furniture, the bollard species is rich and diverse, yet heritage style-codes dictate that one type in particular is installed with greater frequency than any other. The 'cannon bollard' is frequently painted black and modelled on the barrel of cannon. Indeed, early examples are actual decommissioned military cannon, buried vertically in the ground.

BOLLARD MANOEUVRES The addition of bollards to a pavement's edge frequently appears to restrict the walker's movement, reducing the area of pavement that can be trodden by foot. Contrary to common sense, this is not necessarily the case. Bollards afford the walker an easy way to occupy otherwise inaccessible areas of pavement:

Taking the outside edge of the bollard – that is, the edge

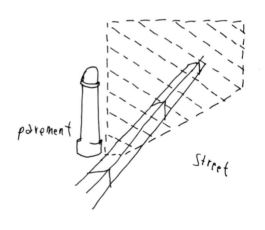

pavement

Street

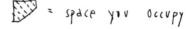 = space you occupy

nearest the gutter – the walker should place their feet towards the edge of the curb, leaning the body out into the road. Such lateral movement at the ankle cannot be sustained for any great length of time, or at such extreme angle without mechanical aid. At this point, the walker should reach for the bollard with tensed fingers, tapping the facing side of the bollard as the body passes. The extra leverage obtained through this movement allows the walker to occupy space otherwise reserved for car doors and refuse sacks.

Fournier Street, E1 [G5 63] is particularly recommended for the practice of bollard manoeuvres, presenting the walker with a range of curb-to-bollard widths on a street of low traffic volume.

d.i.y. stile

A portable stile can be constructed to help you over most fences at roadside or park perimeter.

> This sturdy stile has the advantage of being portable. It can bridge a fairly tall fence. It is not terribly difficult to construct although it may provide a challenge for the beginner.
> Basically, the stile is constructed of 2 x 6s. 2 identical ladders built, then hinged together at the top. A chain passes through the fence to connect the 2 sides and keeps them from spreading open too far. It is wise to tie or wire the stile to a fence post to steady the stile. This stile ... will bridge a fence up to 4-feet high. You can easily alter the height of the stile by changing the dimensions.
> Materials:
> Wood: 3 pcs 2 x 6 x 10 foot or Ladder uprights: 4 pcs 2 x 6 x 55 inches. Rungs: 7 pc 2 x 6 x 16.25 inches. 1 pc 2 x 6 x 8 foot or Rung: 1pc 2 x 6 x 16.25 inches. Top boards: 2 pcs 2 x 6 x 19

COSTERMONGERS AND THE MONARCHS OF WALFORD According to the official directory of Pearlies[14] there is no Pearly King or Queen of Walford, even though the position has been open since 1875. Should the position arise, it would fall to Mark Fowler, as costermonger (from 'costard' [a ribbed variety of apple] and 'monger' [dealer]) to pick up the needle and thread and do the decent thing.

Another candidate would surely be Peggy Mitchell who, as Barbara Windsor, once berated Neasden girl Twiggy in the 1967 song 'Don't Dig Twiggy'. All this palaver would surely have been avoided if Ms Leslie Hornby hadn't waited a further 29 years to release 'London Pride: Songs From The London Stage' – a sure-fire Cockney pleaser.

Walford, London E20, exists for nobody except the Post Office which delivers mail from misguided viewers to the BBC. But for those wanting to walk Walford, it is nevertheless possible to reconstruct it using some simple techniques.

SOME TECHNIQUES FOR RECONSTRUCTING WALFORD
1 Street names
Walford is supposed to contain the following placenames:

Albert Square
Victoria Road
Bridge Street
George Street
Turpin Road

Using a standard Geographer's *A–Z* map, it is possible to ascertain where these placenames are to be found.

Disregarding the instances that occur outside of the East of London and hence beyond *EastEnders*, the distribution b.l.y. stile

inches 2 pcs 1.5 inches x $^7/_8$ inch x 19 inches
Hardware: 16D nails, waterproof glue, 1 pr heavy strap hinges,
4-1-inch screws, eyes, 6-foot lightweight chain or 2 pcs 3-feet
long.

(Hylton 1977: p546)

OTHER WAYS OVER To traverse flexible fencing material such as
barbed wire or vegetation, a coat thrown over the obstacle
will both lower the obstacle and lessen abrasion to the body
or clothing. Sheepskin is a particularly effective material,
being both strong and flexible.

A roll of corrugated cardboard has similar properties and
can be laid over rough surfaces. However, it cannot be carried as unobtrusively as a jacket or coat.

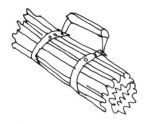

always carry a roll of
corrugated cardboard

or   a sheepskin

linking

the straight track

Bee-keeper, Liberal, photographer and brewery owner, Alfred Watkins understood the worth of the straight line as an aid to navigation. On the 30 June 1921 in Herefordshire, England he became Earth's messenger for the powerful telluric energies that we now know as 'ley lines'. He experienced what can only be described as an *epiphaneia*. Noticing the alignment of ancient monuments on a map, Watkins was convinced that he'd found evidence of forgotten trade routes. These 'fairy chains' described in his book of 1925, *The Straight Track*, he associated with the Greek god Hermes, the god of communication and boundaries, suggesting that they 'decided the site of almost every branch of communal activity'.

Some time ago, the Geo Group in Seattle made an effort to discover new alignments that could help 'balance and tune' the city. What if this could be done for London? Walkers might summon forth and channel Earth energies to counteract those currently in play, those that sometimes act against the interest of the walker.

BUILDING LEY LINES Searching for sources of power or energy involves tracking changes in the Earth's magnetic field. It's possible to build your own ley lines by 'dowsing' for telluric energy, with two pieces of thick wire held in the hands (though the Russian practice of 'bio-location' is supposed to be give more accurate results). Ley lines are typically 70 to 100 paces wide, sometimes doubling in width at sunrise and sunset, as is the case with the massive 'E-line' discovered by Eileen Roche and Gordon Millington. This runs south of London, through Reigate and on to the Isle of Sheppey.[19]

Your first clues will be purely visual: look for conjunctions of obviously symbolic features in the landscape such as hills, churches, masonic halls and the like. There are supposedly centres of energy at Stonehenge and at the Great Pyramid at Giza. By generalising the characteristics of these sites, some have sought to attribute powers to the great pyramid that tops the Canada Tower [D1 80] in Canary Wharf. The London Psychogeographical Association, from the website at the School of Informatics at City University, suggests in 'Nazi Occultists Seize Omphalos'[20] that the pyramid crosses a ley-line that is visible from the power source at Greenwich Observatory [F7 81]. This then leads through Hawksmoor's church St Anne Limehouse [S6 64], the site of yet another pyramid and the object of attention from notable London novelists and conspiracy theorists. The effect of the nuclear reactor once housed in the Naval College [F6 81] at Greenwich contributed no doubt to the 'noxious' energies carried on this line, that should be described not as a ley line but, more precisely, as a 'black stream'.

This 'dragon current' or *lung-mei* can be warped into a low-level path of malevolent natural energy. Seeking energy-vortices, such currents often contribute towards physical and psychic disturbances when passing decaying material (such as graveyards or sewerage-treatment plants) or electrified railways. This does not bode well for the London walker, as the criss-cross of the underground railway network enhances this 'unhealthy energy'.

consumer geomancy

However, this energy from the 'dragon current', whether 'black' or 'white', can be exploited to help in the walking of London. The ancient art of geomancy, related to the spatial and energy divination techniques of *feng shui*, involves scattering earth or other material on the ground, the energy from which generates a pattern that can be read.

A simple adaptation of this technique can lead to fruitful results:

> Method
> 1 Purchase, borrow or somehow acquire a pack of
>   Wrigley's Spearmint Gum.
> 2 Open the packet.
> 3 Hold the sticks in the left hand.
> 4 Hold the hand at chest height.
> 5 Let the sticks fall to the ground.
> 6 Note which way the arrows on the wrappers are pointing.
> 7 Walk in the same direction as the majority of the arrows.
> For added complexity, use Coolmint gum which comes sheathed
> in wrappers with double-headed arrows.

desire lines

'Ideally a desire line follows the line of sight between Origin and Destination'. It is the most direct route between A and B, moderated by obstacles that impede progress by the given mode of transport. When made by those on foot they are most noticeable when crossing large expanses of open space

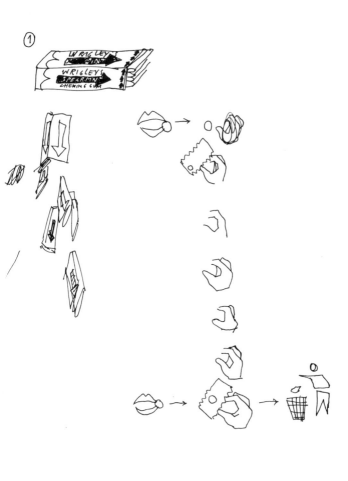

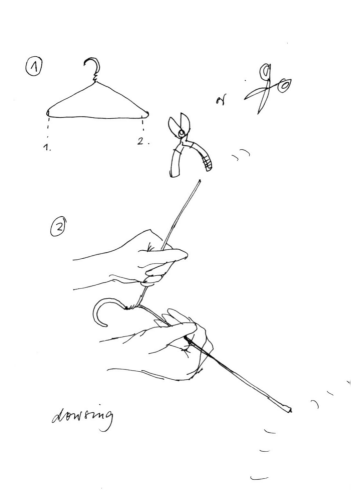

① 1. 2.

②

dowsing

bic biro

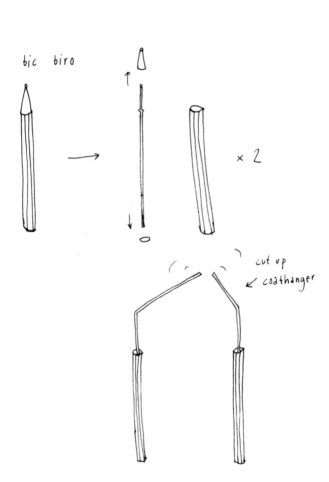

× 2

cut up
coathanger

where they make themselves apparent as worn paths, dirt tracks, dust or mud, depending on the season.[21]

Desire lines highlight the failings of official routes, exposing them as the compromises that they are between the freedom to roam, land ownership and enclosure. When faced with having to make a detour around a park for example, following the path that has been designated to you can rob you of time and energy. In making your own path towards a destination you can give expression to a line of desire, your desire. As an act of solidarity with other walkers, look for lines that have already been cut. Do they lead to your destination? Why not give yourself up to the desire of others?

The network of paths that walkers have made are in danger of becoming 'legacy systems', eventually to be eradicated. Now's the time to make your desires manifest. Go make your mark.

IMPLEMENTED Running from the north-east of Kennington Park, near the corner where Charlie Chaplin once lived, from the gate in St Agnes Place [B6 78], a clear desire line (one of several in this area) leads to the Model House for Families of 1851 on Kennington Park Road. It is particularly noticeable in frosty conditions, 2-foot wide, green on white.

This path is only one of many acts of resistance to be displayed on this turf. Before its enclosure, Kennington Park was common land, frequented by dissenters and rebels.

UNIMPLEMENTED The actuation of desire lines is dependent on terrain and on the obstacles placed in the way of the walker. The city's built environment and its enclosure of open space serves to frustrate our desires – from the shallowest to the deepest – to roam or to move directly.

Even if the physical terrain impedes the actual implementation of our desired lines, there are ways of making our desires known:

1   Define or describe the routes that you desire to take, despite physical limitations. Make this description public in some way. Tell your friends. Tell the council.
2   Desire lines are most noticeable when they are the aggregate of many similar desires. You will need the support of others to make the lines visible and to communicate your collective desire to others.
3   Collect many people's desired routes. Talk with others to find out why they have chosen their route.
4   Pool your collective desires and attempt to realise them. Often many people can achieve more than the individual, for example, walking *en masse* through restricted architectural space or forming human bridges and ladders to scale obstacles.
5   Children are most likely to find direct routes. This is a problem for road safety, but a boon for the development of new rights of way.

open spaces and common land

rights to roam

The campaign for access to open spaces in the British countryside has been active for nearly 120 years. Following industrialisation, it was thought that Britain's population should have access to land 'where health may be regained by bracing air and exercises and where the jaded mind can rest in silence and in solitude' (James Bryce MP, 1892). Movements such as the Ramblers' Association, established in 1935, embodied this emerging *Volksgeist*.

THE RAMBLER The Ramblers' Association, London Office, 1/5 Wandsworth Road, London SW8 2XX (telephone 020 7339 8500; fax 020 7339 8501; e-mail ramblers@london.ramblers.org.uk).

enclosure

It is widely believed that the Enclosures Acts from the mid-eighteenth century set a precedent for land ownership that led to the current state of affairs where the right to roam on open land is limited. Having to support wars in Europe and faced with depleted stocks of grain, the government introduced Enclosures Acts, aggregating land in rural areas to maximise food production. As a consequence of bringing together small plots to form larger enclosures, single landown-

ers replaced the many smaller farmers that had previously
tended the land. The arcane process of bringing an Act of
Enclosure through Parliament was streamlined in 1801. The
Enclosure Act of that year was aimed specifically at enclosing common land. When walking London, it is sometimes
difficult to tell whether land is common or not. One indication should be that larger areas of land are 'unenclosed.' By
contrast, royal parks in inner London, such as Green Park
[FI 77], are obviously enclosed by regal black and gold rail-
ings. But logic defies us when we consider that Wimbledon
Common is unenclosed but not on the register of common
land made by the Greater London Council in 1965.

Many thin strips of land can be included as a single piece
of common land in the register: in Dulwich and Totteridge
for example, there are stretches of common land, verges and
banks, scattered over the local area. This fragmented pattern
of land ownership is one characteristic of current common
lands which hark back to the days before enclosure, of
shared ownership and common access.

common ownership
According to the Ramblers' Association, 'there is *de facto*
freedom to roam to much common land'. However, the right
to roam by all does not mean that common land is held in
common ownership. Much common land is privately
owned, and there can be a tension between those that own
the land and those that wish to walk over it.[22]

FINDING COMMON LAND Part 1 of the recent Countryside and
Rights of Way Bill automatically confers freedom to roam
on any registered common land. Common land is registered
with the local authority.

Metropolitan London's Register of common land is held at the London Metropolitan Archive, 40 Northampton Road, EC1 [A4 62]. Held on site are ledgers recording graphically the location of common land in all districts except those under the Corporation of London's jurisdiction. Under the 1965 Commons Registration Act, the Greater London Council noted all lands deemed as common. Access to these is by appointment only.

The reading room is entered through the antechamber, densely packed by row upon row of grey-haired microfiche scrollers, clattering harshly through large print. After asking at the desk, the large-format 'interscrew' binders' – by London mapmakers James Stanford Ltd of Long Acre, Covent Garden (www.stanfords.co.uk) – each secured length and breadth with flat white cotton tape, are given one at a time to the reader. Pencil only can be used to take notes as you are allocated one of the 40 desks beneath one of the 40 tubular fluorescent lights. Undo the bow, release the tapes, and turn the blue inked edges of the 6 inches to 1 mile maps with care.

Each section of common land is indicated by outlining in green ink, a 'hash' (#) symbol being written adjacent to the outline, followed by a number which corresponds to the Register itself, copies of which are not available.

EXAMPLES OF REGISTERED COMMON LAND
- South end of Rye Lane, west end of Philip Walk. Strip of land in the middle of the road. A traffic island. Fenced with access gate to east, SE15 [G3 95].
- Strip of land between Richmond Bridges [C5 88].
- Shepherds Bush Common, W12 [E2 88].
- Wormwood Scrubs, W12 [C5 58].

NOTABLE EXCEPTIONS

- Wimbledon Common [most of 106], though unenclosed, does not appear on the register of common land at the London Metropolitan Archives.
- Parliament Hill [D3 44] is not common land, though bordering Hampstead Heath, The Vale of Health and West Heath, all of which are marked as common land on the register. The line of demarcation is a borough constituency boundary, marked by a set of boundary stones and posts which runs north-west to south-east, from east of Spaniard's Inn [B1 44] in the north, east of the ponds, towards the athletics track [D4 44] in the south.
- Kennington Park [A6 78], which is, according to Stefan Szczelkun, the 'Birthplace of People's Democracy' and where, 'In reaction to this gathering, the great Chartist rally of 10 April 1848, the common was forcibly enclosed and the Victorian park was built to occupy the site'.[23] The surrounding area, which stretches into Lambeth, was infamous for its popular political activity and entertainment; 'monster-rallies', 'free and easies', the echoes of which could be heard in recent times; the park is still the final destination for many key popular protest marches in London.

royal parks

When comparing the layout of pathways that traverse the royal parks it is clearly noticeable that those which are open to the public feature straight paths, offering direct and speedy carriage for the pedestrian (or cyclist or skater for that matter) from one side of the park to the other. This is in contrast to the enclosed Buckingham Palace Gardens

[F2 77], which offer meandering, elliptical walks, encouraging an unhealthy introspection and other-worldliness in the enclosed royal family.

Terry Farrell's study of royal parks in 1996,[24] which suggests an opening of this and other royal enclosures, proposed a number of gates opening into the gardens: two on to Grosvenor Place, two on to Constitution Hill, and one on to Constitution Monument. This may be a complete misunderstanding of the nature of the relationship between London and its sovereign. Far from demanding free and open access to the grounds of either Buckingham, Kensington or St James's Palaces, it is a widely held belief in some parts that the royal family should be kept 'under lock and key' as it were, permanently isolated. Some of their stamping grounds have fallen into disuse, such as the Grand Royal Axis at Greenwich, a little-known royal route.

THE FARRELL PLAN Terry Farrell also proposes the opening of other private grounds in an attempt to unite the royal parks, linking both Primrose Hill [D1 60] and Hyde Park with Buckingham Palace and St James's Park through opening the straight pathway, down Broad Walk [E2 60] in Regent's Park, through the London Zoo and Park Square Gardens [F4 61] (another site of private, meandering paths) towards The Mall via Portland Place [F5 61] and Regent Street [F6–G7 61]. The other flank of the circular linkage encloses Mayfair and Marylebone as it follows the Regent's Canal, heads south at Little Venice [A5 60] and enters the north of Hyde Park at Marlborough Gate, proceeding towards Constitution Arch and Apsley Way [E2 76], and hence towards Buckingham Palace by way of Constitution Hill.

By coincidence, this walk forces a conjunction of the

memorials to two great British exponents of warfare, the Duke of Wellington, whose museum is at Apsley House at Hyde Park Corner, and Lord Nelson, whose monument stands at the fringes of the walk in Trafalgar Square [D1 77].

HAMPTON COURT PALACE For those walkers who like to roam in what Cardinal Wolsey's Paduan physicians called 'extra-ordinary salubrity', try Hampton Court [A3 118]. Though far from urban, it typifies the unity of park and stately home to which Farrell aspired in his study of royal parks. Farrell himself acknowledges the absence of royal residents at this site, but this should only encourage you to enjoy a stroll in the grounds. Hampton Court Palace and gardens serve as a retreat from Westminster and the City, and can be used in far less structured ways than other royal parks.

FRACTAL LAWNS The lawns to the north of the house are sectioned by regular pathways. On warm days in spring, bluebells stand in the knee-high grass. This is a popular picnic spot; regularly spaced and numbered groups of people play out fantasies of an ideal rural existence in the Squires Meadow, eating bread and cheese before harvest.

slow walks
The pace of walking through grounds such as those at Hampton Court is far slower than in any other situation. Walking at a full tilt in an English Heritage or National Trust property will bring scorn from other walkers. Slow the pace down. This is an unEnglish notion. It contravenes all studies of time and motion, but the slower pace will enable you to walk and talk, observe, relax. You are safe out here, far from the push and shove. Take advantage of it.

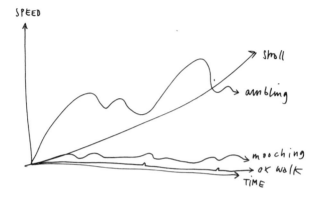

SPEED

stroll

ambling

mooching

ox walk

TIME

slow walks graph

mooching

stroll

ambling

AMBLING You'll need to adopt a relaxed gait; toes out, knees bent and holding conversation. Ambling is not for the loner. Friends or family groups with young children do it best. The amble is often grown into, as a group of people evolve a pace and style of their own over time, compensating for disparities in age and gait and stride and attention span. The group eventually finds itself walking at a constant pace, suitable for all, old and young, fit and unfit, reluctant and enthusiastic.

MOOCHING Disengaged and sometimes malevolent, the mooch is the single-player, omni-directional amble for the bad-tempered. Facing the floor, swinging legs from the hips or scuffing heels on road surface are all tell-tale signs. Favoured by the teen or under-five 'tacker'. Guaranteed to annoy. From the French, *mouchier*.

STROLL Where the amble is a convivial, group activity, the stroll is a quiet reflective category of slow walk. Undertaken singly or in pairs, it rarely involves much chat. It is often a time to reflect or ruminate, or to walk off a particularly heavy meal.

THE OX WALK The ox is a slow-moving castrated bull, used as a draught animal. Little surprise then, that this type of walk is primarily used in the Japanese parliament to delay the progress of bills. A slow walk, it resembles a geriatric conga at best, and at worst the queue for Camelot lottery tickets on a Saturday afternoon. Useful when undertaken by large groups, this walk occupies limited lateral space, making it ideal for narrow environments such as tunnels or corridors.

ancient rights of way

The lowliest order given to those who enter the livery companies, such as those of the mercers, grocers, or drapers in the City of London, is 'liveryman', which confers on the holder, for an extra fee, the Freedom of the City. Entry to the livery companies is through either patrimony, apprenticeship or redemption, where you can buy your way out of slavery and on to the bottom rung of the oligarchy, led by the master and his wardens.

Once the rules of behaviour have been accepted, it was, until recently, the right of any Freeman (or woman) to drive their flock of sheep across London Bridge [D7 62]. But with the price of sheep at market falling by more than 30 per cent per year, surely soon to match the 1327 price of 1 shilling and 6 pence per animal, livestock owners are facing hardship. Unsurprisingly, this right to drove has recently been rescinded to be replaced by the freedom to use the Guildhall's carpark [C6 62] on Tuesday afternoons.[25]

WAYS INTO THE CITY OF LONDON BY FOOT
Roman gates:
Aldgate
Bishop's Gate
Newgate
Ludgate
Cripplegate

Fourth-century gates:
Aldersgate

Medieval gates:
Moorgate

Aldermanbury
Tower
Temple Bar

LATE TWENTIETH-CENTURY 'RING OF STEEL' On foot, it's possible to enter the City unhindered through the police checkpoints, some of which can be found at:

Bishopsgate
King William Street
Eldon Street
Cannon Street
Aldgate

VANTAGE POINTS FROM WITHOUT (with their heights in metres above sea level and direction of view):

- Parliament Hill, Hampstead [D3 44] – >95 metres east and south / into Marylebone and Fitzrovia
- Hampstead Heath – 134 metres / south and east
- Primrose Hill [D1 60] – >65 metres / south and east towards Camden and King's Cross
- Greenwich Park [F7 81] – 45 metres / north, east and west to East End and Isle of Dogs
- Blackheath/Greenwich (General Wolf Road) [F1 97] – 45 metres / west and north-west

ARCHITECTURAL VANTAGE POINTS IN CENTRAL LONDON
- Telecom Tower [G5 61] – central London
- The 'London Eye' [K2 77] – central London and surrounds
- Park Lane Hilton – Hyde Park

- Centre Point [H6 61] – east and west down Oxford Street
- Trellick Tower [5G 59] – north and south in North Kensington
- Canary Wharf [D1 80] – Docklands and east London
- NatWest Tower [E6 62] – City
- East Acton footbridge over A40 [K6 59] – view east towards London
- Vauxhall Gardens Balloon [J6 77] – central London and Westminster

hidden riverbeds

It's possible to follow the geographical contours of London's hidden rivers. Though a high vantage point such as Parliament Hill [D3 44] can be useful, it is often as simple to trace the course of a river when walking. Attune yourself to the changes in contour by regularly checking behind and around you. Often, roads and pathways follow the geographical contours quite closely – look for undulations in the cityscape: hollows, mounds. At others, they may diverge, seeking level ground and making the way for traffic easier.

The tributaries that flow, or have flowed, into the Thames also give themselves away once you know which way the river lies. Obviously, watercourses will find their way downhill, so look for valleys and declines pointing in the direction of the Thames.

A SHORT SECTION OF THE TYBURN RIVER (OR AYE OR SCHOLAR'S BROOK) My walk started in Aldford Street [E1 76], just east of Park Lane. I needed to get to Westminster within the hour, so decided to follow the meander of the Tyburn, if possible, towards St James's Park and the Thorney Island, where the

Houses of Parliament are situated. The Tyburn starts up in Haverstock Hill, but I intended to join it as it neared the end of its journey.

On entering Aldford Street, I headed east, on level ground towards the church on Audley Street, turning right into Balfour Mews and heading across Audley Street on South Street. As I passed the school buildings on the left of South Street the way became undulated and, at the point where South Street merges with Farm Street, the junction on the right into Chesterfield Hill [FI 77] suggested the course of the river. This is a gentle valley, with low banks that tip southward into Queen Street and Curzon Street beyond. Passing Zen Central, I looked for a way through the buildings lining the south side of Curzon Street. The signposts for Shepherd Market take you through narrow walkways into the pedestrian areas of the market. At this point I let prior knowledge get the better of me as I headed left into Shepherd Street and then, as the shops and restaurants appear to run into the blank walls of a warehouse, into White Horse Street.

Once on Piccadilly and looking west towards the road underpass, I could see that I'd misjudged the lie of the land. I was now above the river's course, on its east banks. The Tyburn appeared to run closer to the exit of Brick Street and then across Piccadilly into Green Park's valley.

I dodged across the main road towards the park, entering at the third exit from the brow of the hill and walked in parallel to the river until it met Buckingham Palace. From here, I kept to the east of the gilded Queen Victoria Memorial which now acts as a traffic island and headed downhill into St James's Park.

The pedestrian crossings at this point come under special

control between the hours of 7.00 and 9.00, when normal pedestrian access is denied. The signs show the green man crossed through in red. A warning to us all.

In the park, I followed the path right along the head of the Rosamond's Pond or St James's Park Lake [G2 77] and noticed the trickle of water through the stone embankment standing between me and the palace. This, I guessed, must have been the diverted Tyburn cited in *London under London* (Trench and Hillman 1993).

Leaving the park by the Wellington Barracks exit on to Birdcage Walk, I headed between the two branches of the Tyburn which diverge underneath the palace itself, and made my way across the delta to the water's edge ...

LONDON'S OTHER RIVERS Listed below in the order that they meet the Thames, from west to east. (London Topographical Society, 36 Old Deer Park Gardens, Richmond, Surrey TW9 2TL, UK.[26])

Stamford Brook
Beverley Brook
Parr's Ditch
Wandle
Counter's Creek
Falcon
Westbourne
Effra
Tyburn
Fleet
Walbrook
Neckinger
Shore Ditch (contested)

Peck
Earl's Sluice
Black Ditch
Ravensbourne
Hackney Brook

symbols and way markers

It has long been common practice for travelling people to warn and inform fellow itinerants of their experiences through the use of specialised signage. Scratched on to walls or chalked on to pavements, this can be an aid to the walker as s/he journeys across the metropolis.

The following are derived from Swedish, English, North American Hobo and Boy Scout systems of graphic symbols and may be of use to you on your travels:

- dross
- don't talk at all
- generous women (without men)
- get through this town as fast as possible. Don't stop and be very careful
- accidents and misfortune
- there are dangerous dogs
- irritable people

- visibility reduced by smoke

- go on, they will give

- group is in conflict

- may it be useful

A valuable resource for such symbols can be found at http://www.symbols.com.

USEFUL IMPLEMENTS FOR MAKING TEMPORARY SIGNAGE
For quick 'n' easy, expressive mark-making the following are recommended:

    1 chalk
    2 marker pen (non-permanent)
    3 stick
    4 finger

Very easily marked surfaces

SURFACE	LOCATION	IMPLEMENT
bus	interior	marker pen
	exterior	finger
clothing (coats, jackets, etc.)		chalk
mud	exterior	stick
newspaper		marker pen
pavement	exterior	chalk
train (London	interior	marker pen
Underground, Connex etc.)	exterior	finger
van	exterior	finger
window (dirty, steamy, 'Windowlene'd')		finger, marker pen

walk from east to west, from sunrise to sunset

The rules of the east–west walk:
1 Find an appropriate location to the east of the city.
2 Begin walking westward at sunrise.
3 With reference to a standard Geographers' *A–Z*, keep within the bounds of one row of the map.
4 Break for refreshment whenever necessary. Listen to your body.
5 Stop walking at sunset.

'HOURS OF DARKNESS' Data for 'hours of darkness' can be downloaded from http://www.nao.rl.ac.uk/nao/online/ (HM Nautical Almanac Office).

one instance of the east–west walk
Date: Sunday, 19 December, 1999
Participants: Simon Pope and Matthew Fuller
Start: Canning Town
Delimiter: row 6

Our taxi arrived early and made the journey from Kennington to Canning Town in no time. Our starting point is just beyond where the Meridian line hits the north bank of the Thames, on the A13 as it slips in from the Essex badlands and over the River Lea [G2 77].[27]

If a British December had tilted any other weather option from the array at its disposal, this would have been a daunting walk, but the sky was blue as we faced west for the first time, and the milky yellow fuzz indicated that the sun would make it above the horizon behind us.

7.45. Eleven minutes too early, but it's way too cold to stand and wait. It would be inhuman. The view south is all chrome and steel and taut Teflon, with blue, red and green pinpoint lights; the Millennium Dome sitting, expectant, waiting to be induced in less than two weeks from now; and the factory on Leamouth, which is rumoured to be a food-processing plant. Canning in Canning Town. Too good to be true.

SOUTH BROMLEY The west has been won. Now this, South Bromley, feels like a district waiting to be regenerated, colonised, bought by the new Yuppies, if they're not already here. No more suits, utility wear rules. A new work ethic, hands dirty in media-buying, dipped into other people's expense accounts. From the bridge, a beacon to this potential can be seen to your right, on the Blackwall Tunnel Northern Approach Road [E6 64]: An Ernö Goldfinger tower. Apparently equal in height to his signature Notting Hill address and marking the furthest eastward that any realty pioneer will dare advance.

So, walking westward along the East India Dock Road keeps us within the bounds of row 6 of my *A–Z* map, past 'Ancient Lights' on the right. On the south side of the road, a recently built 'call centre'. This could be any other province: Wales, Scotland. An outpost, a colony, wherever your call is diverted when you phone-bank, tele-shop or remote-complain, a sure sign that labour is cheap and plentiful in the eyes of the telecom industry.

We cross the road and briefly walk down Robin Hood Lane. From where we are, Mackrow Walk looks like it's owned by a foul mix of church and capital or journos from down in the old East India Docks at Canary Wharf cultivating an air of ecclesiastical certainty through German engineering and crystal glass.

POPLAR Already we've deviated from our strict parallel, so we cross back to the north side of the East India Dock Road and head west as far as Duff Street [D6 64].

A gorgeous *faux*-Tudor mansion beckons us northwards towards Grundy Street. So nice to find Reg honoured in such a way after his achievements with *Crossroads* and *Opportunity Knocks*, but the council should have thought again once he'd set sail for Australia and foisted *Neighbours* on us. After all, they revoked the first Mrs Mandela's right to lend her name to public buildings for far lesser crimes.

Further along Grundy Street and on the left stand some remarkable vernacular building projects. This being a Sunday, it feels only right to pay homage to the fine British tradition of do-it-yourself. Marvel at how the rubbish-bin cabins on the right of each house have been amended – and improved in many cases – by the occupants. The farthest house even knocks through this would-be second porch to form an alternative front door, such is the priority given in these parts for speedy delivery of refuse to the local corporation.

An imposing church on the corner of Canton Street, E1 5 [C6 64] marks the way forward. An affiliated school on the north of the street is home to a desolate statue of Our Lord on the Cross. He's pinioned there, on his own, upon a low mound, a de-tubbied Calvary, with only the screaming of schoolkids for comfort. If you're so inclined, this is an obvious photo opportunity: ivy, stone, cross, religious iconography, the works.

LIMEHOUSE We met the tail end of the East India Dock Road

again as we followed Canton Street through an estate over-shadowed by Canada Tower to the south. We're through Poplar now and heading for Limehouse and the junction of Burdett Road [B6 64], Commercial Road and both East and West India Dock Roads. This is the site of one of Iain Sinclair's favourite Hawksmoor churches, St Anne Limehouse. The obvious symbolism of the pyramid in its yard explains much of its appeal, seeing how its form is replicated atop the Canada Tower.

The reason for this church being consecrated some six years after its completion in 1724 is unknown. I have an idea that they waited that long to cross the road, this area being murder during weekday rush hours.

Tower Hamlets, of which Limehouse, Bow, Poplar *et al* form part, is renowned for the rush of public art foisted on it since Thatcher. A twisted metal fence which bounds an area of scrubland is an interesting example and can be found on the eastern corner of this crossroads.

With an ornate funeral directors a few doors away, the café on the north and west corner should have proved too much of a temptation for us. Foolishly, we thought better of stopping for a cuppa and carried on our way, buoyed by the bright sunlight and the by-now refreshing headwind.

Walking on westwards, we passed the The Whitechapel Seamans' Society, where legend has it that the Situationist International gathered in 1960.

RATCLIFF AND STEPNEY Veering north as we meet the rail tracks which run overhead, the old Stepney Station, now Limehouse Station on the Docklands Light Railway, is over the road to the south. We cut up Flamborough Street [A6 64] and into York Square, a BBC drama-producer's dream. Here, there are two small public houses within view, both I am sure, with stock hardmen behind the bar, working for heart-of-gold landladies who just happen to be their dear old mums. This is one of those locations that screams early-years *EastEnders* to you. Watch UK Gold and spot the difference.

The streets round here are rat-runs for drivers cutting through towards Bow from the Rotherhithe/Limehouse tunnel, so beware of chopped Escorts running hell for leather along Salmon and Whitehorse Lanes.

We edge north again, up the south end of Whitehorse Lane until we reach the bottom of the rec next to Stepney Church. It's flying a nautical flag to remind us just how this area was close to seafaring. Salmon Lane itself was named after Captain Robert Salmon, Master of Trinity House, the British maritime authority at the time of the Spanish Armada (Bolitho and Peel 1952: p88).

This is as far north as we should venture, so we go first westward towards Belgrave Street [K6 63], then take a short-cut, 'offroad', straight across the open land towards the John Cass Foundation school on Bromley Street. Here, we walked towards the tower block to our left, morning sunlight picking out its purple painted corporation balconies. By this time we'd realised that this was the colour of this particular Tower Hamlets neighbourhood, having followed a trail of purple bollards through York Square.

We were getting hungry and headed forwards at a pace down Commercial Road. Near the Troxy cinema we waded through a shallow tide of flyers and fanzines. 'The Shoreditch Twat' looked the most promising, though it transpires that this is the author, not the title of the mag.

Around the junction of Sidney Street [J6 63] things get

interesting again, which is hardly surprising given the goings-on in this area, according to the excellent 'Cockney On-Line' (http://www.cockney.co.uk):

> One of the most famous events in London's East End was the siege at 100 Sidney Street, Stepney on 3rd January 1911 apparently involving a Russian Anarchist and a Bolshevik. After shooting at the emergency services, which included the Scots Guards, the two men died when the house caught fire. The film recreation of *The Siege of Sidney Street* (1960) starred Donald Sinden, Peter Wyngarde, Nicole Berger, Kieron Moore, Leonard Sachs and Tutte Lemkow. Sadly, it wasn't restaged in East London, but in Dublin.[28]

We get back on to Commercial Road, using the glare of the sun in the NatWest Tower to keep us on our westwards track.

The Dean Swift pub reminded me of the long trek ahead, a reference to one of Colin MacInnes' ur-Modernists from *Absolute Beginners*, set in Notting Hill at the time of the 'race riots' in the 1950s. Or is it a reference to the equally Protestant Jonathan Swift, author of *Gulliver's Travels*? He was made Dean in 1713 and is connected to this part of town through an acquaintance of his, the rich widow Van-homrigh who lived with her two sons in Bury Street, EC3, just west of here in the City. This was a man taught by William of Orange 'how to cut and eat asparagus in the Dutch manner' – presumably a reference to the 'white asparagus': a vegetable veal forced to grow in the dark, propagated from tissue culture, a male plant from male parents and higher in fibre than any of its green brothers (Swift 1897).[29]

A carpark to house the sports coupés of local council officials has been erected opposite Watney Market [H6 63]. Each floor must be half the height of your average carpark and on this day there were no takers. All gone to Umbria for the Christmas holiday no doubt. WalkIn Fashion, a clothing outlet on the north side of the road, has to get a mention here if only for topicality's sake.

WHITECHAPEL We knew of a small Jewish corner shop nearby which could serve us a breakfast. Turning south off Commercial Road into Cannon Street Road [H6 63] and down on the right on the corner of Burslem Street is Rogg's.

Bear in mind that we walked the walk in 1999: already the famous Bloom's restaurant in Whitechapel Road had closed and very few signs of the Eastern European Jewish community still existed in the East End. Rogg's, it appears, was about to follow suit, due to close in March 2000. I guess there's no call for daily groceries like this round here. The few Jewish inhabitants left are old enough to get the Kosher meals on wheels service and won't make the trek to the cornershop for bagels, lox or some fine cheesecake, and their offspring are off, up north or east, out of it. We bought a brown paper bag full of sweet pastries, with raisins and candied cherries, and high tailed it north again, wishing we could take the owner up on his offer to sell the shop to us, if our bank managers would have it. Transplant this shop into one of the more fashionable districts round here, 'London's Larder' at Borough Market perhaps, and you'd have it made. Where else can you buy gherkins at 70p per kilo?

I took a small notebook with me to record the wheres and whens and it gets me noticed as we get on to Commercial Road again. Someone worse for wear than either of us

glares for an instant and then realises I can't be either undercover cop or DSS snooper because this is before 9.00 on a
Sunday morning and theirs are lazy professions by definition. All that sitting and watching: you can tell by the sizes
of their fat arses and shiny trousers. But since I'm porting a
bag full of cakes, cop can't be entirely ruled out.

We're near enough to Petticoat Lane which will be starting to get busy at around this time on a Sunday, so we shift
north towards Whitechapel Road [G6 63] crossing just
opposite the Worshipful Company of Gunmakers. At this
point, the cakes ran out.

We cut through Whitechapel Lane to reach a set of traffic lights at the bottom of Brick Lane and cross to the north
side of Whitechapel Road, right opposite the cheap battery
shop next to the Whitechapel Art Gallery. Janet Cardiff's
taped walking tour *The Missing Voice*, which begins at
Whitechapel library, is due to end its tour of duty in two
days time, and if the library had been open at this early hour
we might have used her artwork as a further structuring
device for our walk.

JANET CARDIFF: THE MISSING VOICE (CASE STUDY B) You are in
Whitechapel Library. You've been told to go to the crime section.
You hear footsteps. Voices fill your head.
'There's a man signing out a book right now. I'm going to follow
him. Put the book back to where you found it. Let's go.'
For her British debut, Janet Cardiff has made an extraordinary
soundtrack for London's inner city. The work lasts some 45
minutes, tracing a route through Spitalfields and towards the City
of London. The threads of *The Missing Voice (Case Study B)* are
brought to some kind of resolution in a quiet place off
Commercial Street.[30]

Part urban guide, part fiction, part film noir, Janet Cardiff's audio walk entwines you in a narrative that shifts through time and space. Intimate, even conspiritorial, Cardiff has created a psychologically absorbing experience – for audiences of one times as many Discmans as they have at the library, each listened to in isolation. At the library they give you a Discman; you leave the building and find yourself transported back in time. What was that sound? Who is speaking to you? Where does reality end, and where does what's imagined begin?

We hit the corner of Middlesex Street at the back of Aldgate tube and headed north as far as row 6 would allow, which works out to be as as far as Wentworth Street, opposite the red-fronted Suicide Leathers. For a market that according to legend is meant to be bustling early in the morning, it's mighty quiet down here.

We doubled back, taking a westward turn into Gravel Lane, E1. In the 1950s, this whole thoroughfare used to be called Stoney Lane; now it's split into two, reflecting the battle over definition of building-grade rock derivatives that has been played out over the last half century.

We cross Houndsditch next to the Burger King and then across Bevis Marks by way of the cycle lane.

THE CITY At this point I'm on autopilot, this being one one of the ways by which I used to walk to my studio at Clink Street, SE1. Unexpectedly, we wander out of row six and into row five. Passing the black, red and white bollards which signal our entry into the City itself, we cut though Creechurch Lane, cross Leadenhall Street and make ourselves scarce through what looks like a private thoroughfare, Fenchurch Buildings, and down into Fenchurch Street

[E7 62]. We are way too far south by now. We should have taken a right at Fenchurch Street and made our way directly to Bank, but we wend our way in a gentle curve westwards towards the crossroads with Gracechurch Street and Lombard Street [D7 62], known locally as 'Barclay's Corner' from the bank which has a local branch here and which used to have another, for international finance I believe, on the opposite corner, next to the pub.

My phone rang and we stopped on top of a hot-air vent outside Barclay's. I can recommend this as one of the warmest places in the City. The stream of hot air defrosted our feet which by now had suffered the icy breeze for about two and a half hours. It's fun and it's free.

Time for a coffee break. This shouldn't have been difficult seeing as the banks in the City began life as coffee houses. Take a look at the dark blue plaque on the south side of Lombard Street for proof. The site of Lloyds coffee house is pretty much opposite the site of the present Lloyds bank branch. We continued our journey through Lombard Street until reaching Bank [D6 62]. It's worth noting the huge gold locust which hangs outside one of the financial institutions here, a symbol of international capital.

From the end of Lombard Street, the Bank of England is visible to your right and the Mansion House, the official home of the Lord Mayor of London, is opposite. We crossed King William Street, aptly on an amber light, and headed west down Cannon Street and up the hill towards St Paul's churchyard [C6 62]. Still no sign of coffee nor any sort of human life whatever.

On past the site of the Temple of Mithras on the banks of the slighted and banished Walbrook, on past the cathedral, still no coffee. One café was open on the south-facing wall of Paternoster Square, but we decided against going in, holding out for quality above all else. So we carried on down Ludgate Hill [B6 62] towards Ludgate Circus, the junction with Farringdon Street, site of the bridge which once crossed the Fleet river, and made our way up Fleet Street, resolved to find somewhere to rest and drink up west in either Covent Garden or Soho.

HOLBORN For a few years I'd either walked or taken buses along Fleet Street [A6 62]. Once infamous for beer-breathed journos and supposed restrictive trade practices, it is now silenced, having lost out years ago to Wapping and the Isle of Dogs. On both sides of this street, shielded from view behind so many *faux*-medieval castle gates, are the Inns of Court, the spine of which is Chancery, once Chancellor's, Lane [K5 61] which links the Temple to Gray's Inn in the north of this district by way of Lincoln's Inn Fields, where William, first Earl of Craven and Colonel of the Coldstream Guards, rode 'like a madman' policing the riots against 'houses of ill-fame' in the seventeenth century (Bolitho and Peel 1952: p148). The location of the inns is an attestation to how both press and law work as mutual regulators, the excreta of one the staple diet of the other. After a trial separation of sorts, both have reconciled their differences and are 'back in bed' with one another, indicated by the overturning of Lord Archer's claim for libel against a national newspaper.

Our passage out of the City was marked by the oversized gryphon mounted on a plinth which shows its arse to those leaving the 677 acres of the 'square mile'. One of the narrow wooden gates to the south of the street was open, and some builders were on site, dealing with the damage caused to low ceilings: gouges from size 12 stilettos; the smeared entrails of oranges, still concealed in sheer dress-socks, seeping into the floors of the recently inaugurated 'Ally McBeal Single-Sex Washroom'.

We made our way into what seemed to be Temple Lane according to my map, and then further west across what could be Pump Court and undercover through the wooden panelled corridor towards Middle Temple Lane. There were no surprises in here: I think we expected to see in the lead glass and expensive wooden blinds, narrow stairways and cryptic badges of office the equivalent of the Bow neighbourhoods' effort at colour-coded community-building.

If you've ever been behind the scenes at Oxbridge, past the porters and into the colleges and halls of residence, all this will be over-familiar. Which is the point I suppose – an inevitable journey from home to school to college to work. The same courtyards, beadles, cobblestones, seventeenth-century fixtures and fittings. The same outer door kept locked against a chaotic and impoverished outside world. So having lost count of the number of Lambs and Flags on walls, we left, back to the street.

Crossing the road as Fleet Street runs into the Strand – that is, before the traffic island dedicated to the church of St Clement Dane [K6 61] of nursery-rhyme fame – just about kept us in within row six of my map. The gentle incline up Aldwych, the site of the bus bomb of 1997, takes us past the front entrance to the London School of Economics and opposite the monolithic façade of Bush House, the spiritual home that the BBC deserves. The students invited fellow BSc Economics student Mick Jagger and his Rolling Stones to play at the LSE in the 1960s. During the succeeding decade, the Sex Pistols played the Royal College of Art, one of their first public performances. Fatboy Slim is rumoured to be playing sometime soon at North Benfleet Institute for Life-long Learning.

Bush House stands, in itself, as a slice of Great Britain's brain as it was structured from the 1920s to the 1950s: 'Nation Shall Speak unto Nation' runs the byline of the BBC. In practice this is interpreted as 'London and students of English from Oxbridge shall tell everyone else what to think and how to enunciate clearly and precisely'. This was carried out not just by the British Broadcasting Company, as it was way back then, but also by the Secret Services, who camped-out in offices on the eighth floor of the northwest wing of the same building. It was pure coincidence that MI6 chose to house the Z Organisation, an intelligence service known as 'London Film Productions', here.

Even more of a coincidence was the Special Operations Executive's decision to station its political warfare executive at Bush House during World War II. Broadcasting 'black propaganda' to Europe, it won the praise of Goebbels for its ability to demoralise a civilian population, a skill maintained by British broadcasters to this day.

With the Indian High Commission next door, you have a powerful triumvirate capable of everything from minding the empire to snooping and culture-control, all under one roof. A one-stop shop.

COVENT GARDEN On the eastern corner of the junction of Kingsway with Aldwych we discovered a close competitor to the hot-air vent found in the City earlier in the day. Hungry, thirsty and chilled to the bone, we stood and thawed for a moment, then marched across Kingsway, past the Waldorf Astoria Hotel and north into Drury Lane. Our main objective was still to reach a decent coffee shop, and we were confident that the Old Compton Street branch of Patisserie Valerie would be open for breakfast at this hour on this day of the week.

Cutting down into Covent Garden itself by way of the left turn into Russell Street next to the Peabody housing estate, we had ducked very slightly out of the sixth parallel, so headed quickly north past the early-start buskers and licenced street entertainment. Crossing Long Acre [s6 61], we shifted downhill and into Shelton Street then into Earlham Street for the climb to Seven Dials. At this tight junction of seven roads a couple of local sun worshippers were clocking the sundials that run round the top of the column in the centre of the road, undamaged by the ravages of fire which ran amok through the warehouse offices in Earlham Street in the late summer of 1999, 333 years to the day since the last Great Fire.

Throughout the day there had been talk of inferno and tragedy. In a nearby Moroccan restaurant, one floor down and packed tightly with leather cushions and chalked walls, a woman had been called away, her house on fire in another part of town. Meanwhile, the owners speculated upon what might have happened if the electrical fire at the back of their fridge had taken a stronger grip. Nearby, friends of mine who live here thought it was their boiled rice on fire, went outside when they realised this was more than a domestic disturbance, only to return to burnt rice. A tragic set of circumstances.

Carrying on down Earlham Street we were stopped by a bloke who was rummaging through some bins for food. I was nearly delirious with low blood-sugar at this point, so when Matt gave him some cash, I pointed out it would have been a better idea to trade for the tasty sandwich he held in full view. I refrained from stealing it off the poor sod, and knuckled down to the short walk across Charing Cross Road [H6 61], Cambridge Circus and into Old Compton Street by way of Moor Street.

SOHO This put us squarely in W1. Observing the very British, rule-bound nature of this walk, we had to find coffee and cakes within the first part of Old Compton Street, before the junction with Dean Street, so here we are at Patisserie Valerie as planned.

We take a seat, fashionably near the door for the toilets. Things have changed slightly since I last asked for a *citron pressé* and some *petits fours*. They've put a second floor in and lost one of the tables downstairs in the process, making room for the flight of stairs. We order coffee, orange juice and almond croissants and take the weight off our feet. It's about 10.30 and we're joined by what appear to be Stateside ex-pats tucking into smoked salmon and eggs-over-easy, on toast.

We stay for about half an hour, noting which body parts hurt most. Matt's knees are causing problems and I've got a weird pain in the outside of my right hip. We decide on a path that'll get us through Soho towards Oxford Circus and set off at a slightly slower pace than we'd established back in Canning Town.

Taking a right out of the shop and then north up Dean Street, we cut through next to Gossips westwards to Wardour Street. Travelling north again, we pass the MGM building Hammer House, which I have never noticed in all these years of traipsing up and down here. The Hammer House of Horror, suitably appointed opposite the Mezzo restaurant, is site of many a last supper and death knell to script development, production contract and between-the-ranks office romance.

We head into D'Arblay Street [G6 61] and cut through to Poland Street and then Great Marlborough Street. Crippled by the prospect of walking through the West End and not going shopping, I demanded at this point that we head towards the recently established Nike Town outpost on the Oxford Circus frontier. Getting there from here takes us past the northern end of Carnaby Street and the arts and crafts frontage of Liberty on our left. We take a right on to Regent Street at Dickens & Jones and find ourselves in the crowd of Christmas shoppers down for the day to marvel at the similarity of the layout of Boots stores in Oxford Street to those in Wolverhampton or Guildford. Not a word from any of these expectant punters, hushed, glazed, ripe. No shops open and it's past 11.00. The queues of the preceding days had made the national news.

Tips for shoppers: 'go in the shop and look for bargains', says a leading shopping advisor. So the Sunday girls and boys are inside, finicky hands pulling at millennium party dresses and rejigging the stacks of monochrome boxes of overpriced aftershave which will soon have 14-year-old gel-haired, fast-food freaks gawping, leaking into their Kappa easy-care tracksuit trousers.

Nike Town still closed, we cross the north to the north of Oxford Street towards Hennes, and, catching the slipstream, are flung at a pace further westward through this shopping paradise. Some people hate it, but this is quality shopping territory. Too bad we couldn't nip into the revamped Top Shop back on Oxford Circus. It, along with Selfridges at the western end of Oxford Street, is enough to fill any Saturday afternoon with bargains or high-priced prizes. With all else in between, there's something for everyone down this way. We head towards the brow of the hill and then down the slope, deciding to take the turn north into Gees Court, signposted for St Christopher's Place [E6 60], so as to make a direct line to Paddington and beyond.

MARYLEBONE The north side of Oxford Street has many secrets, St Christopher's Place being one of the least well-kept. This area was legendary in the early 1980s, Vivienne Westwood's Nostalgia of Mud characterising the 'hard times' chic which got up the noses of the rest of the nation at the time. There's still the Toni & Guy hair stylists' school and innumerable branches of the London School of Fashion dotted around here. If you head further north you get to Marylebone High Street, now Dale Winton territory, but still grand in some ways. We take a sharp left towards the public toilets in the pedestrian section of Barrett Street, cross James Street and head towards Selfridges.

In this part of town, it's worth looking for the short cuts through department stores, as they usually take up corner plots and can save miles of wandering and diversion if you're on a shopping or walking mission. Selfridges covers a considerable amount of floorspace on this corner. I would have preferred to cut through the ground floor by way of the Miss Selfridge annex and headed towards Orchard Street through the high-class food hall, always a treat. But the doors are barred. More panic over the provincial hordes out to queue for the day, egged on by the prospect of news coverage of their voracious pre-Christmas ruck.

The reciprocal processes of art and fashion continue to enjoy each other's company, judging by the flat vector graphics which adorn the Miss Selfridge window. Julian Opie's show at the Lux in Hoxton Square during late 1999 showed straight-up, bored, slightly agitated cut-outs, mutely demanding attention from passers-by. Younger, increasingly bored versions of the same stand larger than life in signal colours at the party-for-the-end-of-the-world on the plate glass facing Duke Street. 'I get no kick from vodka Red Bull'.

Swinging north up Duke Street we take the next left alongside what was known by some employees of the US Signal Intelligence during World War II as 'Selfridge's Annex'. Beneath the low-rise exterior to the north of Edward Mews lay four or five floors of voice encryption and listening devices which monitored Churchill and Roosevelt's telephone link. Other intelligence services might also have been housed there. (Berkeley 1994: p182) This site may be above the tunnels which carried the GPO's telephone wires. Just maybe.

Further north and west of here can feel dull when walking: wide pavements and one-way drivers seething at one too many sets of traffic lights. We rush through it as quickly as possible, speeding along Orchard Street, north into Portman Square and west into Seymour Street [D6 60]. We get fed up with the monotony and cut across towards Berkeley Mews.

Don't be put off by the whiff of affluence that clings to every pastel-coloured wall..Mews are less congested with traffic than the main streets they once served and are always useful shortcuts.

An access road immediately on the left opens into the back of The Bricklayers Arms. We didn't feel the over arching need to drink at this point, being more concerned to hit Notting Hill and food at around 12.30.

TYBURN AND PADDINGTON We're into Upper Berkeley Street, taking a left towards Edgware Road, the first part of the ancient Watling Street (Bolitho and Peel 1952: p149). We cross at the traffic lights into Connaught Street [c6 60]; beneath us Tyburn Brook. We skirt the posh frontages of the north side of Connaught Square, the site of the Tyburn gallows. The purple gazebo, the concealed entrance to a tunnel erected as part of a twinning exercise with Stepney, stands in the private gardens here.

Shocked from our musings by the sight of an old lady in a towering husky-hair wig, we continue towards Hyde Park Square. If you're down this way, check the high-class butchers on the right of the Connaught Street. The sausages look good, but chandeliers on the first floor are sheer and inappropriate decadence.

At this point I found that my sense of direction failed badly, for the only time on the whole journey. This can be partly attributed to being unfamiliar with the territory. But even when I could see the gates and outer fences of the north of Hyde Park, I couldn't make sense of my orientation. When referring to the map I couldn't find our location easily, so I resorted to the compass.

Mercedes territory. We take a right, north, and follow Hyde Park Street into Hyde Park Crescent. Here, the imposing church at the focus of the crescent was thronging with children on mobile phones, a testament to the excellence of network coverage in this part of town. The church has apparently no real claim on its extensive tracts of land in Paddington. The monks of Westminster laid claim to the fields here in the eleventh century through forging documents of ownership. This only confirms our fears and we take note of the 'Tradesman's entrance' signage and disap-

pear into Somerset Crescent and then north again into Rad-
nor Place. Despite *Paddington Green*, the BBC's soap-u-
drama, this area stinks and we get through it as quickly as
possible. Across Sussex Gardens [B6 60], up towards Praed
Street, beneath which the Irish Fenians detonated a nitro-
glycerine bomb in 1881, by way of Norfolk Place and hang
a left towards Paddington Station.

If you've never tried crossing on double mini-round-
abouts before, let this be your baptism of fire. On the Burger
King side of the road, cross towards the station. Look for
cars and buses trying to knock down and injure tourists of
every nationality. Get yourself into the service road that runs
to the right of the station, to its east. Nip down here into the
station itself and you'll be out of traffic for some time.

Paddington Station was renovated during 1999 and now
boasts numerous coffee shops. Maybe it was the fear of
dehydration, or just that food and a sit-down in Notting Hill
were less than half an hour away, but we briskly made our
way over the concourse. This had been a poor day for
celebrity spotting, until now. We walked past the bloke who
used to be a mechanic in *Coronation Street* and was in the
Flying Pickets – you know, the short one with the outsized
sideburns. He was in *Twin Town* too, and was no doubt
heading back to South Wales that very day. We make
towards the Eastbourne Terrace exit of the station, over
towards the outsized bronze of Brunel, levitating above a
very low plinth, symbolic of where the nation now considers
both public transport and engineering in its estimations.
There's a taxi lane which runs immediately at the foot of the
stairway that you'll need to take. Be more cautious than I
was at this point: I strode into the path of an oncoming
white 5-series BMW and forced the driver to slow suddenly.

Even though I was on the crossing, it's an informal interpretation of the standard pedestrian zebra crossing and the driver had trouble drawing the same conclusion as me as to the correct etiquette to observe.

BAYSWATER Heading up the steps into Eastbourne Terrace [A6 60] put us at the site of a border skirmish of sorts. To the north the open fields, fresh air and grouse moors. Monarchs of the glen. To the south the greed, the filth. Parliament. At the junction with Bishop's Bridge Road, into which we turn left, there's a street sign that has been defaced – 'The Royal Borough of Barnet and Islington' added into the available white space – gillies from the Deer Park at Kensal Rise, angry at the annexation of this sliver of land by Westminster Council, having made the careful alterations late at night: high on acorn brandy, smeared in rabbit excrement, draped head-to-foot in freshly culled elk hide.

NOTTING HILL It's downhill from here for a while: further west, Bishops Bridge Road melds into Westbourne Grove [K6 59], and most residents would call this Notting Hill. This is 'Westeburn, a hamlet that lay "west of the stream"' (Bolitho and Peel, 1952: p149), but has nothing in it to remind you of the hanging tree. Overtaking the bloke pasting call-girl cards neatly into all the phone boxes, we race towards the junction with Queensway, indicated by the third great dome of our walk, Whiteley's, so nearly Hitler's official London residence, away on our left.

So now the only focus was on food. Our walking injuries were playing up as we made our way up the incline after crossing the Queensway junction. We figured on stopping for noodles under the Westway on Portobello Road, so we ignored all the eateries that we passed. Of all the places to get food of any persuasion on a Sunday, this must be it. Everywhere else seemed to be experiencing some form of prohibition in comparison. Where Westbourne Grove hits the wide curve of Pembridge Villas and Chepstow Road [s6 59] we continued westward along the front of the Brazilian coffee shop to carry on along Westbourne Grove towards Portobello Road. A right turn at the Portobello Road [H6 59] junction takes us north again and we head as far north as we can go according to the rules, that is, to the Westway, raised high above our heads. This is a key aid to navigation in this part of town, being visible from the northern face of Notting Hill. Unfortunately, the noodle shop was shut, and we made our way back up Portobello Road to a curry, chips and beans shop on the western side of the road.

We ordered: chips and beans for Matt, bacon, egg and chips for me and two cans of Coke. No toast. By now it was obvious that if we walked at this pace, we could make it as far as Reading by sunset. But our knees weren't going to hold out. It was 12.38 and we needed a plan if we were going to survive. Not wanting to finish Matt off completely, having invited him without knowing the full impact that this walk would have on the body, I suggested that Ealing might be possible and scheduled a stop at a pub along the way. The least I could do. So we resolved to carry on. It would only be three hours until sunset anyway, and we'd been out for nearly FIVE hours already.

So we left the Daytime Café, Nightime Tandoori and made our way west, with a right-hand turn, in bright sunshine, into Westbourne Park Road. The pubs on every corner were open, but empty. I've heard that all of Notting Hill takes its 4 x 4 down to Wiltshire or Oxfordshire or wherever on a Friday night and doesn't come back until the eve of the working week. It was true that we'd not sensed too much affluence out walking today, mainly New Zealanders on low-budget tours, but we passed our first local with obligatory dark glasses as we turned right into Ladbroke Grove [G6 59]. We crossed immediately and headed slightly north to meet Lancaster Road. Hanging a sharp left, being careful of the ice that was still glazing the pavements, we made our way past the rise and down Bartle Road towards Silchester Road [F6 59].

This was an area made famous to a few by Colin Macinnes' *Absolute Beginners* but nothing's left to testify to the accuracy of his description of the place. The 'west cross route' of the M41 bounds it to the west, the Westway, the A40(M) to the north. The indigenous trees, after years of fume sucking, have developed their own self-regulation: pollarding. Stark, grey against the sky.

The junction of Silchester with Bramley was again disorienting. A wrong turning left took us past one bullbreed leading another; no irony, no nothing, just a dog on a lead as an excuse for people to shit themselves. So we faced north using the compass and looked for a way over to Latimer Road [E6 58] and the safety of row 6. Rather than walk by roadway in a loop via Oxford Gardens, we crossed to the west of Bramley Road and followed the pedestrian footpath that mirrors the reinforced structures holding the Westway. The artificial turf of the football stadium is at eye level as you follow the path to its left towards the climbing centre. Walls with moulded foot- and handholds compete with the highways department for the best view of the traffic and a bleak basketball court holds two frostbitten addicts, shooting hoops one-on-one. Check the long-jump pit – the runway gated to introduce a new element of skill into the game. Opposite is a wildlife garden, struggling to filter oxygen from the dense traffic fallout.

Years of frustration at having such limited access to the open sky have been vented by launching footballs at the overhead roadway. Pale pockmarks freckle the charred underbelly of the Westway, bringing down the light in 6-inch disks.

NORTH KENSINGTON Right under the tangle of sliproads that signals the intermingling of Westway with the M41, the footpath bears right into the southernmost tip of Latimer Road. The western sky opens, horizoned by the railway track, and we have the feeling that we're leaving 'inner London'. The streets are cleaner here; the eastern side of the road being residential, the western side light commercial, service sector. Low-budget television companies with a beady eye on travel and gardening commissions peer enviously at those more-established producers and directors over the road, dining in a pub conversion, a French restaurant, where the tanned and the grey dream of leaving the business altogether now the secret's out in the open. This is a long road, and in bleaker weather could break even the most hardened walker. But we take heart at the sight of cars and shops ahead, the first signs of life, running perpendicular to us, east to west.

High-cheekboned blond women in second cars reckon on the upper part of Latimer Road as a safe place to park-up and make that urgent nail appointment on the mobile. A related species of young men gather in the New North Pole pub on the junction, miming loudly while engaging in open-plan drinking. Many a fast buck has been made from pub and restaurant conversion in these parts; start-up interiors changing like the westerly wind that whips in from the hinterland to our left, and here's proof. We've made it to another landmark: the North Pole pub. Beyond here, icy wastes and the detritus of failed and futile acts of bravado. Few get past here alive. North Pole Road [E5 58] is short and spans the railway beneath us as we inhale sharply and make a final dash, looking for a place to rest. Up ahead is the Pavilion pub, servicing the housing estates on the edge of Wormwood Scrubs and other residents of Wood Lane.

Inside we get beer. London Pride seems an appropriate choice. We're hurting pretty bad by now but are distracted by the warmth and the novel sensation of being stationary. This place is rammed full of old geezers ordering Sunday lunch. They don't seem worried by the millennium countdown clock beaming its red diodes at us. Twelve days, ten hours and 28 minutes.

We spend some time in here; an easy thing to do on the best of days, but with another hour and a half to walk we make every excuse not to leave. We don't buy a second pint though, and make some decisions about the next part of the route.

Leaving the Pavilion and turning south down Wood Lane we pass the house, on the corner of Glenroy Street, of someone who seems to be getting in some early practice for preparing Christmas dinner: binding all their topiary in clingfilm and aluminium foil. Peacock, lion and duck, all ready wrapped. Fit for a king.

This street corner is also remarkable for having the dirtiest postbox in London, or at least in W12.

EAST ACTON AND THE BEGINNINGS OF SUBURBIA We cross into Ducane Road [E6 58], next to the expanse of the school playing fields. The ice is still thick out this way, making the going treacherous underfoot. It suddenly gets colder, the sun is low to our left. On past Hammersmith Hospital [D6 58] and past the building site at the front of Her Majesty's Prison, Wormwood Scrubs [C6 58].

Here's where we start to notice the end of the urban. We've been used to high-rise until now. No front gardens. No semi-detachment, and we feel uneasy. Both of us having come to London from smaller towns and cities, we know what it's like to feel hemmed in. That this overwhelming desire to escape hits us outside the west quarters of the Scrubs should surprise no one.

All types of media have zoned in. Miffed at how much press attention their sons and daughters are getting as chore-ographers of dinner parties for friends of top-rank celebrity chefs, instigating dependencies on cocaine and immaculate disposable clothing, they shifted the emphasis to the suburbs and a life more ordinary; the great 'people show' next door. It's being described nostalgically, softening the blow when the time comes and the family arrives. Out of Hoxton back to Surrey, or Middlesex or wherever. Lauded as the incuba-tor of new musics and youth cultures, the suburb reeks glamour for the watery-eyed jaded hack, mid-30s and still not through their teens. Memories. A return to the young and dependent. Steal their youth. Bath in their radiance. Burst their bubble. If the suburbs have an energy, it comes from those wanting to leave, propelling themselves out of here or living fantasies of the same. A last gasp before pre-mature death or zombied acquiesence. For those resigned to stay: coming to terms with a long and dull life and never leaving your school friends. Forever the fattest in the class.

So our walk gets less thrilling; a rattle of bones, black

cloth and scythe. A tap on the shoulder. There's no one there.

We walk the rest of the road, the arts and craft-influenced semis and detached houses browning out an otherwise vibrant day. The shops at East Acton sit high on the bank above us as we approach, the church, an altar to prime real estate, smack in the centre of them. This place is a by-pass; no stopping. Dull. We'd be walking into the sun if it wasn't hidden behind the hill we're going to have to walk up. We decide against taking the main Oxford Road, saving our lungs for the journey left up Brassie Road [A6 58]. The council estate opens before us, small patches of grass behind sagging, tight steel-mesh fencing and hip-high concrete posts. We get a funny look from a bloke and his missus at the top of the hill. Beady eyes putting a stop to any malarky with his Sierra. A greyed, veiled house at the junction makes sure we quicken our pace downhill, back towards the Oxford Road [K6 57]. We're looking to make a crossing as soon as we can and stumble on a pedestrian footbridge that'll afford us a decent view. We're quite a way uphill now. The view back east from here lets us track our movements right from Docklands. The sky is clear and bright, picking out Canada Tower and Centre Point, enabling us to orient ourselves perfectly. A look at the compass tells otherwise: pointing in all directions as we walk the length of the bridge, the magnetic force of Acton confusing matters; a vortex careening through the suburbs. You are here and here you'll stay.

On the handrail, a recurring theme on this journey, a paean to the demise of Blood and Honour and the dangers of reckless motorway driving. From this vantage point, putting the world to rights, railing against the foreign, incomprehensible metropolis. So close you can smell it and so small you can hold it in your hand. Crushed, dashed on to the windscreens and the river of steel below.

THE END: WEST ACTON The houses get larger; an estate where your relatives live, Matt reckons. Private. Quiet. We make our way through the maze of under-used pavements and tread moss for the first time. A footpath to the right of the Scout hut takes us into Emmanuel Avenue, merchants' houses, red brick, white detailing. Mostly single occupancy but a tally of white vans reveals hidden rock bands and Christ Army factions behind closed curtains. Acton. Home of guitar bands. The Who in waiting. The Action in repose. Downhill towards the main road and signposts to Acton mainline.

We're tempted. Very tempted. But we push on past The Leamington and towards the row of drive-in retails. The Viagra sign, written large and visible to passing reps, prostates pummelled by unyielding Vectra upholstery.

The car is loaded with cheap wine from the off-licence as we pass and swoop left into what we know to be the final road we'll walk this afternoon. We're on the opposite side of the road to the huge brick church and we pull our gaze up from the floor and towards the horizon, scoping for signs of West Acton tube station [G6 57]. We discuss the possibility of pushing further towards Ealing; we know we're running TEN minutes early, but we can't do it. We're broken, demoralised by the unrelenting semi-detached streets; the oversized Acton playing fields with their too-cheerful call to local team-players and swarthy tennis masochists.

Even the unusual raised pedestrian crossing fails to lift our spirits. We trudge, defeated at the last, towards the Japanese mini-market at the top of the road. We pay our

£2.40 just ten minutes before sundown, catching it reflected in the cruel disfiguring concave of the tube carriage as we duck back under White City, back to the urban to nurse our wounds.

EALING AND BEYOND Given more guts and stamina, we would have ended up at North Ealing tube station by sunset. Best of luck to you. But if you can get past Hanger Lane and you still need a guide, I can recommend Patrick Keiller's film *London*. Fast forward to the final section that features the River Brent Park walk. It runs outside of my rules, too far north, but it'll give you a way to skip the suburbs altogether and get into the rural.

road traffic

what is traffic?

A question overlooked by even the most experienced walker, the government's 'Let's Decide – Walk Wise' scheme recommends that you make distinctions between the following for your own safety's sake.

Learn to be aware of the differences between:

- things that move/do not move
- things that belong on the pavement/on the road
- different colours
- different sizes
- different shapes
- various speeds (fast and slow)
- different directions of movement (near/far, coming/going)
- different noises.

Awareness of your relation to traffic and the environment can be enhanced through:

- comparison of your size with that of vehicles and road environment (best done in a car park. Could be done with moving cars, though not recommended)
- comparison of hard/soft (compare yourself to a car)

- moving model vehicles at fast/slow speeds (running down slopes of various degrees)
- listening to sounds, loud/quiet
- comparison of how much can be heard by stopping and listening with how much can be heard when moving.

the rule of the road

Unlike most autocentric countries, in Britain drivers of road vehicles must 'keep left'. If you are new to London, keep reminding yourself of this. At some pedestrian crossings you will see 'look right' or 'look left' instructions in white lettering, painted on to the road surface. They apply to you, so consider yourself warned. In areas heavily serviced by public transport, such as Oxford Street [D6 60–H6 61], beware of emergency vehicles running contra to the rule of the road. They have the law on their side to some extent, though recent press coverage of the supposed SIX people per day injured by wayward vehicles flashing blue lights has served to temper their driving habits.

types of driver

It is important that you get to recognise the types of driver out there. They come in many shapes and sizes, from all parts of the globe, each with their own particular habits and psychoses. However, once in London, *en masse*, certain behaviours emerge as drivers interact with each other and their surroundings.

MAYBE IT'S BECAUSE ... You might think that the car careening across filter lanes is driven by a local inhabitant, warped and deranged from the dense and inhumane living conditions, brain starved of oxygen from birth by the South Circular.

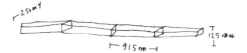

You are wrong.

Panicked as soon as the M4 runs into the Great West Road, the oncoming swerve driver is displaying a provincial approximation of the Londoner's mind-set: aggressive, defensive, self-obsessed to the point of being a pint-sized psychic black-hole. In no way are they the real thing. Be thankful for this. They are scared and alone. You are only alone.

One way to tell the difference between a real Londoner and the scared shopper from out of town is by running a cursory MOT test over the enclosing car. Failure of test = near-integrated migrant. Full-on write-off = the real deal. Much of London's wealth was made from waste collection of some sort: surplus currency, surplus resources, surplus excrement. Offer them 50 quid for scrap and feel part of this city's perpetual Dickensian fantasy.

Born of industrial and class conflict, the road vehicle wants to make sure that you stay in your place, arresting your movement at every opportunity and dissipating your energy. If the twin cities of London and Westminster have survived it is because of their ability to regulate flow: people and money, natural resources. Surveillance cameras and traffic-light systems now control the through-put of road vehicles; in turn, pedestrian flow is regulated through inter-action with the road vehicle.

Unless there is little or no traffic on the road – during a right royal funeral for example – your walking will be interrupted as you wait to 'give way'.

WHEN TO GIVE WAY There are people who won't stop; not for cars or lorries or buses or bikes or anything. This issues a head-on challenge to the road vehicle. Now that Britain is catching on to litigation for even minor accident and injury, maybe I should revise my opinion somewhat, but I still consider this to be a dangerous performance.

Generally, roads are where things that are bigger than you travel faster than you. Therefore road junctions have the potential to bring together extremes: hard and soft; fast and slow; the quick-witted and the stupid. I'm taking it for granted that you know where you fit in this scheme.

DRIVERS BE WARNED The zigzagged area at marked pedestrian crossings are also controlled areas for drivers and you have the right to cross here. *The Highway Code*, published by the Department of the Environment, Transport and the Regions, has this to say to drivers about your rights as a pedestrian crossing the road:

> Road junctions
> 146 ... Watch out for pedestrians crossing a road into which you are turning. If they have started to cross they have priority, so give way.

THE HIGHWAY CODE While the code itself does not have the force of law, many of the rules in the code are legal requirements and people who disobey those rules are committing a criminal offence and face prosecution. *The Highway Code* may also be used in evidence in court proceedings (MacDonald 1999).

crossing

crossing the road

You walk the line, the line between flesh and steel, from the safety of sovereign territory. On the pavement little in the way of harm can be done to you. But all good things must come to an end and you will surely arrive at an intersection with road traffic.

Prepare to cross the cultural divide ...

where to cross

Three situations:
The government's own 'Let's Decide – Walk Wise' identifies three types of road crossing situation:

- places where visibility is restricted, for example by a bend, a brow of a hill, or parked cars
- places where traffic is coming from several directions, for example crossroads, т-junctions, driveways and car park entrances and exits
- protected crossing situations, for example zebra, pelican, subway, footbridge, pedestrian refuge (island) in centre of road, crossing controlled by school crossing patrol/police.[31]

OFFICIAL RECOMMENDATION The safest and most regulated place to cross is a protected crossing, the zebra or pelican for

Ⓐ slight

Ⓑ very dangerous

accident

instance. If you can't find one of these, find a place where you can see traffic and drivers can see you.

Never underestimate the danger of a parked vehicle.

BEWARE THE WHITE VAN BEARING GIFTS A particular danger is presented by parked delivery vans. At certain times of day, during the early morning in particular, London will be teeming with white vans. They'll park anywhere, blocking pavements to gain easy access to shops and offices throughout the city. They will not only obstruct your view of oncoming traffic as you attempt to make a crossing, they will also force you off the pavement and into the road. A common mistake when such a situation is encountered is to try to squeeze through the slightest of gaps between wall and van, only to be hit by cargo as it's off-loaded from the back of the vehicle. This can happen if the van is approached head-on and you lose the advantage of being able to see into the back of the van to the person unloading it.

FIND A SAFE PLACE
   'In each class of 30 children two will be killed or injured in a road
   accident before their 16th birthday.'

This is because some children think that if they don't see the car, the car doesn't exist. Naïveté won't save you from high impact. See the car and then decide whether or not you want it to see you. In some circumstances, taking the silent way to remain invisible is necessary for survival. But as far as straight-ahead vanilla 'crossing the road safely' goes, make sure to 'see and be seen'.

STREET GAMES The street was once the site for much impro-

→ people trying to touch

→ people trying to cross the street

chuck Norris

①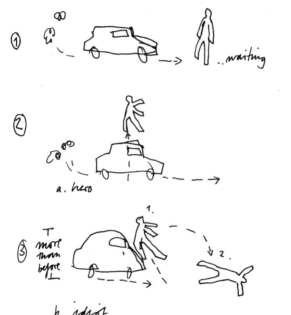
...waiting

②

a. hero

③ T
more
than
before

1.

↓2.

b. idiot

vised game play. Since most road accidents and fatalities involving children now occur on residential streets this tradition is in decline. Games such as British Bulldog were played between, and structured by, the flow of traffic, as were innumerable other variations on the 'hit' or 'it' game.

Being told once too many times to 'go and play with the traffic', many of us turned to the game of Chicken where players dare each other to run ever closer in front of the moving vehicles as they pass. (Note: play Chicken at your own risk.)

One recent development of this game has been the 'martial art' of car jumping. This is essentially a game of Chicken played perpendicular to the normal direction of play, where a high vertical jump takes the player over the oncoming car. With the introduction of tall 'people movers' such as the Ford Galaxy or vw Sharan to the streets of Britain the popularity of this sport is declining as more players face enforced retirement through serious ankle injury.

the six types of protected crossing situation

1 Zebra

> 'A non-signalised crossing indicated with black and white stripes across the carriageway with Belisha beacons on black and white striped poles at the carriageway edge. Drivers should give way to pedestrians on the crossing.'

2 Pelican

Pedestrian-operated signal crossing. Lights (eventually) change after pressing of button located by the crossing. Includes audible (or rotating tactile indicator) during green man. Signals show flashing amber to cars after red – during this time pedestrians on crossing still have priority but 'new'

pedestrians should not cross the road. Peds see a flashing green man at this time.

3 Puffin
Advanced Pelican with possible microwave detectors and pressure pads to modify signal timings. Devised to avoid the problem of signals on Pelicans changing after the pedestrian who pressed the button has already crossed. Good idea but the technological problems have not really been overcome.

4 Toucan
Combined pedestrian/cyclist signal crossing. Otherwise as Pelican.

5 Pegasus
Combined pedestrian/cyclist/horse crossing. Otherwise as Pelican.

6 Pedestrian facilities in junction signals
Signals at junctions often include either a pedestrian phase as a normal process of the cycle or a ped – on demand only. Will not include audible warning but should now include rotating 'knurled knobs'.
From *International Pedestrian Lexicon*[33]

the golden rules for using a zebra crossing in London
1 Thank Mr Belisha
The British government has been kind to the pedestrian. With Leslie Hore-Belisha's beacon we were given our first taste of mastery over vehicular traffic.

In most regions and provinces of the British Isles it is common for drivers and riders of road vehicles to abide by the rule of the road and to 'give way' to any pedestrian already on one of these crossings, or to those who have entered into the 'zigzag' zone which delimits it.

In London, it's the same game, but with different rules. You may believe that you have the 'moral and legal right' to be on the crossing but drivers will think otherwise. For them, you're fair game. You will have to compete with them for space on the road. If the only space available is beneath the bull-bars of their 4 x 4, then so be it.

2 Make eye contact
Drivers in London – anyone in London – will not be used to this. As the mongoose holds the gaze of the cobra, you must be resolute and strong. A moment's indecision can leave you just another crossing casualty; a notch on the leather-bound steering-wheel; a fly speck on the polarised windshield.

3 Wait for the oncoming vehicle to slow down. Never attempt the following numbers 4–7 while a vehicle is accelerating or shows no sign of slowing.

4 Use hand signals
While approaching the crossing, gesture clearly but subtly that you have acknowledged the driver's generosity in slowing at a pedestrian crossing. ('Flipping the bird' is not recommended, even though US research shows that you may be the recipient of such a signal from drivers.) Whether they stop or not is another matter.

5 Look in both directions at once
Look both with and against the flow of traffic. Taxi drivers and couriers of all kinds, together with certain emergency

back

side

services, have assumed the right to ignore the rule of the road as observed in the British Isles.

You will not appear to be a foreigner if you follow this rule just as long as you make your final 'traffic check' to your left, towards the flow of traffic. You should now see a rapidly slowing vehicle which is preparing to let you cross the road.

6 Maintain an even stride
Road users will want you to get the hell off their road as soon as you can. Do not loiter and make sure you have the gait of someone who knows where they are going.

7 Beware the blindside bicycle
Most of us have been cyclists at some time. The image conjured up by former prime minister John Major of old maids wobbling along on iron-framed bikes, basket brimming with freshly baked loaves and bottles of warm beer or gin, flows tsunami-like through the English psyche.

Dream on. Cycling in an urban environment depends on the individual's pain threshold and an ability to summon up deep anger. Anyone who can spend the day lathered in their own sweat is worth staying clear of for many reasons.

At least cyclists are now liable to £25 on-the-spot fines, even from traffic wardens, if caught peddling on the pavement.

being visible
The issue of visibility has been well worked over by academics, artists and activists alike. Even Burt Reynolds (http://www.burtreynolds.com), star of *Smokey and the Bandit* and *Boogie Nights*, has been in on the act with his

Vision Express television adverts.[33]

Making ourselves visible to the gaze of authority can be hazardous; but making ourselves invisible to oncoming traffic can be terminal.

REFLECTIVE CLOTHING In recent years, everything from designer catwalk uniforms to the diversely branded running shoe have featured silvered reflective future-fabrics. Footwear manufacturers have been particularly unrestrained in the use of this new material, applied in strips angled to make the wearer visible from the side or rear. This has its advantages if you want to be seen at night or in poor visibility by those who are outside your own field of vision. London is mostly well lit by street lights, traffic headlights or the glow from its multifarious shopfronts, especially so in its central and inner districts, so this technological breakthrough might prove superfluous if you are wary about who's watching you.

BE DECISIVE It is better to make yourself seen when it suits you. When you need to come into contact with traffic, make yourself known with confidence and drivers will respect you for it. Londoners know that hesitation is a sign of weakness and, like the lame wildebeest, you'll be savaged by the wild dog if you display it openly.

how to cross

DO AS I SAY: KERB DRILLS Kerb drills form an important part of a child's induction into the ways of the walker. Take this opportunity to refresh your memory and to review the historical developments of these codes of conduct.

As an extension of the 1936 government guidelines,

ROSPA's 'Kerb Drill' of 1942 was aimed at lowering the high child accident rate: 'Look right, look left, look right again; when all is clear, quick march.'

Interestingly, during the height of British militarism and the uniforming of the nation *en masse*, this seems to vindicate the continuing *jihad* of pedestrian against road user. Tufty's 'Green Cross code'[34] has similarly been rewritten. The following is again culled from the 'Let's Decide – Walk Wise' scheme and provides the urban walker with some useful guidelines to crossing:

- the kerb is where you stop before you cross the road
- keep away from the kerb, i.e. stay on the pavement
- always hold hands
- walk steadily
- do not run, play or dawdle
- recognise that vehicles can come very close and sometimes mount the pavement.

TUFTY CLUB Tufty the squirrel taught many under-fives the rudiments of road safety, appearing on television, and in books, teaching packs and poster campaigns. Here are some Tufty facts:

- Tufty 'Tufty' Fluffytail was born in 1953
- Tufty appeared with many other characters including the 'persistently naughty Willy Weasel'
- Tufty Clubs, a nationwide network of local groups organised by ROSPA, were formed in 1961
- at their peak there were 24,500 registered Tufty Clubs around the country
- Princess Michael of Kent accepted an invitation to

become the club's first president
- the Tufty Club newsletter was later known as the *Tufty Times*
- the Tufty principles are as firm today as they have always been.

This and more information is available from Cotswold Collectables' website.[31]

Tufty lost out however, when road safety education moved away from 'accident reduction', based on statistical analysis, towards the 'relief of intimidation, fear, anxiety or danger';[35] a move from 'child-centred survival instruction to curricular integration'.

As Gerald Cummins points out in *100 Years of Road Safety*:

> The 1936 report on schoolchildren had an earlier 'kerb drill' which was very similar to the later Green Cross Code, viz:
> Always stop at the Kerb.
> Always look Right, then Left before crossing.
> Always keep a Careful Look-out while crossing.
> Always look out before stepping into the street from behind a Car or Omnibus.
> (a) Where possible, cross at Traffic Signals, Islands, or other Marked Places.
> (b) Wait for the Clear Signal, watch the Corner for turning Traffic, Then cross.
> (6a) Always walk straight across.
> (6b) Never loiter when crossing.[36]

the kerb

It is often presumed that 'the kerb' is as easily defined as it is understood. The US Access Board's report on 'Accessible Pedestrian Signals' includes the following valuable information for those concerned with the boundary of pavement and street.

In times when physical barriers between nations and peoples are rapidly being dismantled, it should come as no surprise that the 'kerb ramp' is being introduced to aid in the merging of pedestrian with vehicular traffic. With little effort blind pedestrians, for example, are able to occupy the same space as other road users. The main drawback of the kerb ramp is that there is no indication, through the walker's sense of touch, when a transition has been made between the pavement (a place that is safe), and the road (a place where you can be run-down and killed).

In Britain, the shortcomings of the 'kerb ramp' were lessened by the introduction of tactile pavement surfaces at and leading up to the border zone itself. Small, raised truncated domes are positioned within a catchment area to minimise the risk of a pedestrian entering the street before having realised the pavement has ended.

kerb construction
All paved surfaces which are known as 'flexible' in the trade

– whether of flagstone, gravel or Tarmac – need to be edged in some way by a kerb-unit. Where they meet the road, they are within the jurisdiction of the local authority's highways department and are subject to their exacting standards.

A J McCormack & Son's web resource details every aspect of kerb construction.[37] Refer to BS7263 for specifications for precast concrete flags, kerbs, channels, edgings and quadrants.

kerb profiles

There are four basic profiles of precast concrete road kerbs used in London:

- they are usually 915 mm in length
- 'tall' kerbs are approximately 125 mm x 250 mm or 150 mm x 300 mm
- smaller units are approximately 125 mm x 150 mm or 150 mm x 150 mm
- special transition kerbs are used to link two differing kerb profiles? such as at 'dropped crossings' where pedestrians may cross.

Special care should be taken by walkers when negotiating kerbs that have been affected by tree roots. In 'Roots and Routes: Guidelines on Highways Works and Trees' by the Department of the Environment, Transport and the Regions we are given some indication of the common repairs undertaken on kerbs damaged by root growth that result in non-standard kerb profiles:

- reducing the kerb section
- creating a gap in the kerb to accommodate the root

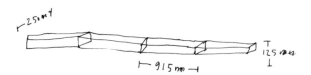

25mm

915mm

125mm

imagine between
walls is the sea

kerb hopping

- bridging the kerb over the root; or
- constructing a kerbside build-out.

Kerbside build-outs are particularly difficult, carrying secondary risks for the walker such as drainage anomalies.

the limits of the kerb

To familiarise yourself with the boundary between kerb and road, try these few practical exercises from 'Let's Decide – Walk Wise' with your friends:

- use the edge of a mat as the kerb; discuss where to stand (or use a chalk line marked on the floor if no mats are available)
- point out the danger of standing too close to the edge
- play games, such as musical statues, where you dance to music and stop when the music stops or at the sound of a vehicle. You could follow directions connected with speed and movement
- try different kinds of movement: walking, hopping, skipping, running, dawdling. Discuss which is the safest on the pavement.

HOLDING HANDS Why not try some more forms of 'hand holding' on the crossing?

- invite strangers to hold your hand while you cross the road
- hold hands with strangers without their permission. Guess their destination and guide them safely towards it
- rather than hold the hand of just one other person as

would you
like to
hold my hand?

you cross, form human chains that stretch from one side of the 'kerb ramp' to the other. An average of five people linked in this way can form each row. The deeper the rows the better. For one of the widest pavements, go to the Mile End Road [B3 64], and use the pedestrian crossing just on your right as you exit the underground station. On this stretch of the A11, pedestrians are given up to four times the amount of space normally allocated to them.

- likewise, form a chain across the road, reaching the entire width of the available carriageway.

Children will be used to forming these 'crocodile' formations, so it might be useful to ask one of them for the very latest tips and tricks. The crocodile formation is strictly defined as a column of units, usually pairs, where each person of the unit holds hands with the person adjacent to them. Vary the width of unit for variation, environmental conditions or just for fun.

PLATOONING The 'platooning space' at an intersection (US Dept of Transportation 1999: p53) will attract a wide range of pedestrians, not all of whom will have your level of skill or ambition as a walker. Many will be bemused by the breadth of choice afforded them by the crossing of the road. Some will be disoriented. Others will just be slow. Either way, to avoid frustration, make sure you get into the front row of crossers and stay there. If the front row seems to have reached capacity, look for the wide angle and extend the line laterally. Or grasp the opportunity to avoid platooning altogether and make your way to the outside of any railing that skirts the kerb ramp area. In this way you might find a way

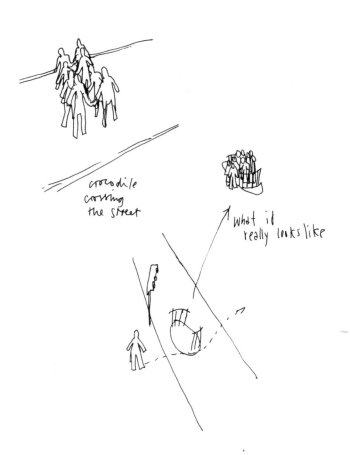

crocodile crossing the street

what it really looks like

AVOID PLATOONING

of truncating the designated crossing zone altogether; pass across the extremities of any 'splitter-island' or median area.

crossing velocity

The rate at which you cross the road depends on where you cross, who you are, and who else crosses with you. Some places where we might want to cross are obviously biased in favour of the motor vehicle. Any time we approach a clearly delineated kerb with no kerb ramp or marked crossing the chances are that road traffic will have right of way. In this situation, you must attain a high crossing velocity and a high rate of acceleration from start-up. A study published in the US *Road Engineering Journal* shows that one third of all pedestrians can achieve only 90 per cent of the average walking speed. Their lead-in time – the crucial time taken from an indication to cross to start-up – is also regularly underestimated by the planning authorities. So most pedestrian crossing situations, even designated ones, are likely to leave you at a disadvantage. Don't get caught out.

Walking speeds
Average walking speed of able-bodied adult = 4 feet per second (1220 mm/s). Pedestrians who use wheelchairs typically travel faster than this
Average speed of those with mobility aids, gait or stamina impairments = 1.5 feet per second (455 mm/s)
Transportation industry research in the US suggests a more conservative walking speed of 3.1 feet per second.[38]
(All figures from US Dept of Transportation 1999: p88)

traffic control symbols

Increasingly, the 'red man' is depicted in confrontational

mode; hands on hips, appearing to lean forward, about to hector a motorist awaiting a green light, evoking the spectre of the car-jack. Even the neutral Swiss pictogram has been infiltrated by the new spirit of intolerance.

other pedestrian crossing systems

THE BARNES DANCE The Barnes dance is a crossing system that gives unprecedented power to the pedestrian. At an 'all red' phase of the traffic lights, the walker has right of way in any direction, including diagonally across the road junction. This is the 'dance'. No more having to cross two flows of traffic to reach your destination. London can proudly boast of absolutely no such crossing systems, but we can wait in hope. It seems that only Denver, Colorado, where former traffic commissioner Harry Barnes developed it in the 1950s, has fully implemented the system. Harry later moved to New York. Unfortunately, his gift to the world is less well travelled.

THE FOOTBRIDGE Footbridges afford the pedestrian passage over many of London busiest roadways. Many have both deep- and shallow-stepped access, some are of spiral design and most are contructed of steel. Newer models will have been built to minimise vibration.[39] In doing so, the manufacturers will have set an upper limit for pedestrian load and made a study of the resonant frequency ranges of materials used. From these figures, acceptable limits of vibration will be ascertained, even under full-on 'vandal loading' conditions. Footbridges only encourage vandal-like activity of course, being positioned so accurately above passing traffic.

Those footbridges on the hills to the north and west of the city typically offer wide panoramas of the metropolis, sitting tight down in the Thames basin.

There appears to be some correlation between the view and suicide rate, footbridges with full vistas being likely to have a higher incidence of self-harm activity. The 100-year-old Archway Bridge over Archway Road (the A1), one of the earliest of London's footbridges, forms the boundary between the Hornsey Division and Holloway Division North Sector of the Metropolitan Police, who note:[40]

> This bridge has an infamous history due to the number of suicides. Unfortunately for Holloway Officers, of the suicides that take place there, nearly all take place on the south side of the bridge which is part of Holloway Division. This is believed to be so, because the south appears higher and the view covers the whole city of London.

Archway Bridge is also known to the local civilian population as 'Suicide Bridge'.

a law unto yourself
In many urban road-crossing situations you will encounter an endless stream of traffic, frustrating every attempt you make to cross in a 'by-the-book' manner. At this point you will have to improvise and play with the rules a little.

JAYWALKING ROSPA conspires with Mayor Rudy Giuliani of New York City, imposer of on-the-spot fines, when they say: 'Jay-walking is a dangerous practice that all pedestrians should avoid. Education and publicity are likely to be more effective counter-measures to this problem than legislation, which would be difficult to enforce'.

Jaywalking does, however, formalise the activity that we take for granted; namely, crossing the street where you

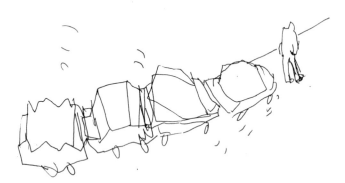

Ed Nelson

shouldn't. Learn to love it for all its liberating qualities:

> *Jaywalking* This term stirs up strong reactions among pedestrian activists. Dictionary definitions imply that there has to be danger, traffic and carelessness. Mid-block crossings are NOT synonymous with jaywalking. Asserting right of way is NOT jaywalking.
> *International Pedestrian Lexicon*

The Morris Dictionary of Word and Phrase Origins (second edition 1988) says that:

> Jaywalker dates back to the early part of the century, when jay was a popular slang term meaning 'countrified' or 'rustic'. A farmer, strange to the ways of the city and perhaps frightened by the new-fangled automobiles churning down the streets at fantastic speeds up to fifteen miles or twenty miles an hour, might have been expected to cross the street in an erratic fashion, without paying too much attention to signals. Hence, jaywalking.

DANGEROUS BUT EFFECTIVE Ted Nelson, guru of Hypertext and master strategist,[41] apparently invented a new way to cross the road while at Harvard: 'when arriving at a busy road, he would dramatically turn his back on the traffic and step with theatrical nonchalance off the pavement. Drivers, frightened, would slam on their brakes', writes Gary Wolf in 'The Curse of Xanadu' (*Wired UK*, June 1995). With litigious pedestrians a known danger to US drivers, this reaction is understandable and may explain the rapidity of their evasive action. Drivers in London are far less likely to see you as a threat, so temper your implementation of this technique.

TRAFFIC DENSITY CALCULATOR One of the most important

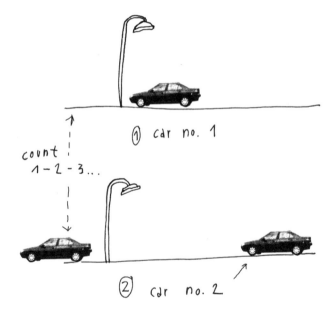

① car no. 1

count
1 - 2 - 3...

② car no. 2

skills you can acquire is that of judging the rate of oncoming cars. This will give you information about braking distances from which can calculate whether it is safe to cross.

Method
Select one particular oncoming car from a steady stream of traffic; note when it passes a way-point such as a bollard or street lamp.
Count for three seconds and if the following vehicle has already passed the waypoint, the cars are moving too fast. Choose another way-point, further away. Check the timing again. Wait until the gaps in traffic flow is at least three seconds before attempting to cross.

FENDER DODGING When traffic is slowing to a halt, for example at traffic lights, aim to walk close to the rear end of a stationary or slow-moving vehicle. Knowing that most drivers will want to avoid contact with the rear of another vehicle, the foot or so behind a stationary car is an assured safety zone. You can walk deftly across any road using this technique.

Showing that you understand the driver's mind set, that you know before they do that they'll have to apply the brakes, is invaluable in the constant battle of wits between pedestrian and all other road users.

KNOW THE FLOW You're in Wardour Street [H8 61], heading west. Maybe you've just been to a swanky media party somewhere. At Mezzo perhaps. The K Bar is a fair bet. You want to cross the road but you're a little the 'worse for wear'.
Question: What's the first thing that you should do?
Answer: Know which way the traffic flows. It's not an

uncommon mistake in Soho to look one way, see no traffic and then step into an oncoming taxi or motorcycle courier.

The only way is to memorise the direction of traffic flow. This is recommended if you are going to be a frequent visitor to a certain part of town. If you plan to be on first-name terms with London's post-production houses you'll need to know the flow patterns of the several north–south passages which run in parallel across this district. Greek Street, Frith Street, Dean Street, Wardour Street, the half of Berwick Street which isn't a market, and Poland Street will all stand in the way as you make your way to the first floor of Liberty's by way of its Great Marlborough Street [G6 61] entrance, to blow your wages on Comme des Garçons shirts (Pope 1998).

Soho flow
Greek – south
Frith – north
Dean – south
Wardour – north
Berwick – south
Poland – north.

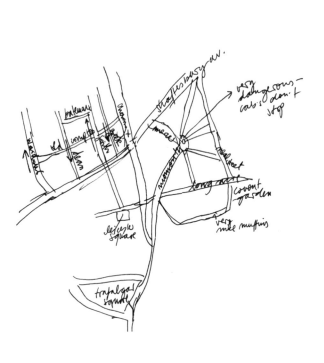

rush hours

Remember that the 'city that never sleeps' is New York; London barely drags itself out of bed for work. Rush hours here tend to be later in the morning and earlier in the evening than in other British cities.

personal space

In contraflow traffic it may be necessary to assert your individual right to pavement space. Weaving and sidestepping oncoming commuters is tiring and distracting so you may want to try some of these techniques:

USE OF MOBILE (CELLULAR) PHONES IN CONTRAFLOW Whether you have an urgent call to make or not, phones should be carried in the hand at all times of peak pavement traffic. In contraflow situations, the raising of the elbow as the phone is shouldered into call-making position excuses the use of the humerus as ramming device.

Highly recommended for use in areas with high rush-hour flow rates such as Oxford Circus. If you don't get your blow in first, you stand no chance.

CHEST AND SHOULDER BLOCKING Choose your target carefully: someone of your own height and weight walking towards you.

Do not deviate from your path.
Keep walking at a steady pace.
Be of even balance.
Make no eye contact.
Wait for impact.
Aim to get hit on between upper chest and shoulder.
Never look back.

the rush hour as machine for memory

In contrast to places such as Los Angeles where, according to the Venice Beach grafitto 'history is myth', Westminster and London are twin cities of memory. While their everyday concerns are for systems, flows and a clean passage-to-exit, they have a need to store traces of human activity – traces of such things as conversation, reflection, conflict and attrition. Over time, cities produced machines to restrict flow and to increase the possibility of sedimentation. The rush hours are one such instrument, in much the same way as the ebb and flow of tides leaves debris on the seashore.

For pedestrians, there is a massive deceleration as crowds are forced into ever more-confined spaces: roads, bridges, tunnels, stairs, tube trains. Once speed is decreased and proximity is increased there is a massive potential for inter-personal communication; a potential that is only rarely realised. The most common form of dialogue is seldom made public however, a bitter hate campaign conducted as soliloquy in the privacy of each human brain.

the underpass

Many of London's 'multi-exit' pedestrian underpasses are clearly signed for your walking convenience. Many conform to a graphical standard that indicates all the exits by number, on a very small-scale map of the local area. Tube stations often deploy similar signage and it is possible to generate walks of your own from these numbering systems, should you value chance and gameplay over utility and purpose.

Method (note: you will need a coin)

1 Find an entrance/exit and an exit map to ascertain the number of the exit that you have chosen, for example 5.

2 Look for the highest number on the exit map, for example 7.

3 Subtract the lowest from the highest number.

4 Head for exit with the resultant number. This gets you started, etc.

walking in underpasses

The rule of walking in underpasses is to move quickly and with purpose. Underpasses are no place in which to loiter, as they rarely suggest a meandering path. They are usually constructed in short, straight sections, joined at right angles and designed to convey the pedestrian as quickly and as directly as possible to their destination.

marble arch

There are 14 exits to choose from at Marble Arch [D7 60]. Number 14 itself is on the north side of Oxford Street at its junction with Edgware Road, and it was here I began my own journey. Many of the outer corridors are decorated with monochrome, highly glazed mosaic and contain the shells of makeshift beds, abandoned for the day to be reclaimed at night. Large, square, heavy-duty McDonald's cardboard boxes are popular, as are bread crates, repurposed as bedsteads. On one particularly cold day in February, there was relatively little wind-chill to be experienced, but the low light levels and futile, pale fluorescent lamps made life uncomfortable. I'd determined to reach exit 7, which took me first back above ground, at the point where the routes for 1–7 and 8–9 deviate. The 6-foot x 6-foot floor tiles indicate a flight of steps to the surface, into the space allotted to the arch itself and a row of fountains, today at rest.

It is impossible to sit in the zone surrounding the arch itself as the pigeons have laid waste to the benches.

THE MARBLE ARCH LABYRINTH The Marble Arch underpasses are a superb example of this utilitarian plan. Softened in places by the humanising effects of mosaic and explication board, there are zones of rest and of passage. There is no evidence that there should be any commingling of the two however. Rest is taken above ground, passage is made below. There are some exceptions, most notably where there are signs of makeshift bedding, evidence that the architectural scheme can be reinterpreted at ground level by its users. Less obvious is the way that you can explore the underground sections of this complex at leisure.

Towards exit 7, there is a set of grey double-doors that

appear to lead to an area of restricted access. Behind these doors a tunnel stretches for several hundred yards. Wander aimlessly through these corridors and you will find hidden exits. Follow the signs for petrol alongside the car-only exit ramp. Take the short flight of steps through the green double-doors with reinforced-glass panels and you will emerge, blinking, into Hyde Park through a door marked 'emergency exit only'.

light and dark
Steps into underpasses drop in short flights, falling away sharply from the sun into a half light. On bright days, the walker can experience a moment of blindness as their eyes struggle to adjust to lower light. Older walkers are especially prone to this.

In this situation, care must be taken by the walker: concentrate on placement of the feet. It is easy to miss a step and tumble. Pay attention to the surface underfoot; feel for the edges of the steps.

Wearing sunglasses accentuates the problem as both relaxed pupil and dark lenses increase the difficulty of adjusting to the new lower light levels. And remember that 'nystagmus' or 'rapid movement of the eyeballs'[42] can be experienced when walking in poor lighting conditions, as it can in 'glare'.

GLARE When light shines in the 'wrong' place it is considered to be 'glare'. In areas of highly contrasting light values there is always a danger of 'disability', 'discomfort' or 'reflected' glare.[43]

typical light levels

Be prepared for considerable variations in light levels which are, according to the TUC's *The Workplace (Health, Safety and Welfare) Regulations 1992:*

> Very bright daylight – up to 100,000 lux
> Overcast conditions – 30,000 to 40,000 lux
> Shady room in daylight – 100 lux
> Street lighting – 20 lux.[44]

crossing the river

why cross the river?
To get to the other side.

You might be walking to work, meeting a friend, carrying a placard, but sooner or later you'll find yourself crossing the river. Since tolls were lifted, it has cost the walker nothing to use any of the bridges that cross the river. The same applies to the few foot-tunnels that lie downstream. The Thames flows roughly west to east; a natural division, yet another boundary to be drawn.

north vs south
Londoners are famously and endlessly engaged in the debate: north versus south, the border between being drawn by the silent River Thames. A facetious question in the My London section of the *Evening Standard*'s Friday 'Living' supplement asks: 'When did you last go to south of the river?' It's as if south London's a backwater, off the beaten track, somehow disengaged from the cultural and financial machine that was most recently the focus of 'Cool Britannia' and was once epicentre of 'Swinging London'.

Black cabs are rumoured to stay clear. There are too few tube stations. It's flaky and homespun. Too comfy. Too self-satisfied. Technically it's Surrey, after all.

It's like the suburbs but closer. And they have those barmy local-council members, still coming to terms with Mrs Thatcher in their cheap, slubbed suits.

The north is where the rich admit to living. It's got the City and the West End. It's got the East End for that matter. Its influence is so strong that it even claims bits of the South Bank as its own. Why do you think they built the Millennium Bridge [C7 62]?

When walking, you'll be in the most advantageous position possible to judge for yourself how each side of the river feels. It's easy enough to keep an open mind if you're a visitor but if you're a resident, it may take some time before you chip away at the prejudice that blinkers you.

the thames

The River Thames remains strongly symbolic to Londoners. It suffered many years of abuse, choked by years of outflow from sewerage and industrial process. The regeneration of its banks, whether realised in full or forever arrested at the Lilliputian scale of the architect's model, followed the cleansing of the river itself and its reinstatement as life-force of the city. Many guidebooks feature sections of this walk, satisfied to have reunited the citizen with the river.

OFFICIAL RIVER WALKS The official Thames Path runs 294 kilometres (183 miles) from a field north of Kemble in the Cotswolds to the Thames Barrier in Woolwich. It splits at Teddington, offering you the choice of walking through London on either the north or the south bank. The Ordnance Survey's 'Explorer' maps[44] indicate the route of the Thames Path as it makes its way into and through London.

bridges

PEDESTRIAN ACCESS With the exception of some railway bridges, the bridges that cross the Thames are accessible to pedestrians. You will find that many bridges give you access from the riverside as well as from the main roads that cross them; look for stairways built into the side of the bridge's structure. These are often found on both north and south ends and east and west faces of the bridge, but are not always easy to spot. Some, such as Waterloo Bridge [K7 61] have open, visible steps on the south bank; you can see from a distance other walkers making their way to road level. But some, such as London Bridge, have obscured and intimidating stairways on their south sides. Tackle these with an air of certainty. They can be daunting places to negotiate, often with dark corners which seem to swallow sunlight.

official use

London's bridges serve certain accepted functions for the city, its inhabitants and visitors. The present London Bridge [D7 62] and its predecessors were built on the only obvious crossing point in the lower reaches of the Thames, the banks there being sufficiently stable to hold any construction. The other bridges over the river were built in subsequent years for both convenience and necessity, the type and frequency of their use depending on circumstance.

The new crossing at Bankside, for example, does not respond to the demand of traffic flow. It is constructed to stimulate economic and cultural regeneration and to force a cohesion between two dissimilar districts of London. Its site is determined by politicians and to some extent the inevitable tumble to the south implied by the steps from St Paul's to the river [C7 62].

It can be useful to know how these bridges are used; as a walker you will need to moderate your behaviour according to the many situations faced. Most bridges force adherence to their official role as a means to transport bodies from north to south, but some are open to interpretation. Hungerford (Charing Cross) Bridge [KI 77] is often used for fly-posting or stickering as well as for more traditional activities such as begging and busking.

things to do on london's bridges
look at the view ... throw things over the side ... television interviews and adverts ... walk to work ... take a rest ... watch boats ... demonstrate ... impale the heads of traitors ... sing into the wind ... find the resonant frequency of its structure ...

BRIDGE SLALOM Start on the approach to a bridge, from either north or south bank, facing towards another bridge. (This bridge can be either up or down river.) Cross the bridge and make your way to the other bridge. Cross it, leave it, and head towards the next bridge. Continue this zig-zag across the river.

Add further structure to your walk. For example, place a time constraint on the activity or determine in advance the number of bridges that are to be crossed. You could also walk until you are exhausted, or resolve to walk every bridge from Tower Bridge [FI 79] to Hampton Court [A4 118].

look at the view
Some of London's bridges afford spectacular views of the city. Waterloo Bridge for example, occupies a central location and is excellent for views both east and west. The foot-

path on Hungerford Railway Bridge [K1 77] has two viewing points where you can step out of the flow of pedestrian traffic and look eastward at your leisure. Here there are also good examples of captioned 'skyline' information boards which help the casual viewer to pick out the recognised landmarks from the panorama.

On the busier and wider bridges such as London Bridge [D1 78] you will regularly see tourists taking self-portaits with the city serving as backdrop. They will always be stationary and may cause obstruction or even total arrest if they ask you, the oncoming walker, to take that shot for them. Like jury service, you'd better do it out of duty, knowing that one day you could be the one in need of impartial assistance.

THE BRIDGES AT NIGHT Most of London's bridges are illuminated from below; some, such as the Chelsea [F6 77] and Albert [C6 76] bridges, are covered in lightbulbs along their upper structures.

THE SKY Much of central London's streetscape shelters the walker from the elements and obscures the sky. Bridges are a place to reacquaint yourself with these simple things and sometimes offer a speedy transition to open vistas. In other cases, such as at Westminster Bridge's northern approach [J2 77], the sensation is similar to nearing the seaside: the view opening gradually as it falls away into the tide.

London skies are bitten through with a sulphurous yellow which reveals itself as a brown nicotine rash when approached from neighbouring counties. Nevertheless, when you've been locked into close combat with car fumes and barging shoppers all day, it can be a relief to get out on the middle of one of the quieter bridges.

flow of workers on bridges

At certain times of day – the rush hours when the tide of commuters from Kent, Sussex, Surrey and Hampshire hits the mainline railway stations at Waterloo, London Bridge [D7 62] and Charing Cross – the bridges leading into the City are rammed full of workers, rushing forward, panicked into silence.

This single, sensing body is sometimes unfairly described as a frenzied, cornered rat gnawing at the exposed flesh of global economics.

If you're on London Bridge, at 9.00 or 9.30 for example, you will find the flow is from south to north. The tide turns in late afternoon as offices close and everyone heads for home.

useful techniques for 'city' bridges

WALKING WITH THE FLOW It is generally held that to be walking with the flow you must be on your way to work. Probably not of high rank (you'd have a chauffeur by now), you should wear grey, so as not to be anything other than in the crowd and with the flow. This is an important rule; apply it uniformly across all areas of your life.

If you're not a commuter, for pity's sake, learn to look and behave like one if you find yourself among them. They are the silent majority we all fear. Provoke at your peril (especially on Friday nights).

You may find it useful to invest in some specialist equipment to carry, wear or brandish when walking with the flow on City bridges.

UMBRELLAS Black, fox-framed and cane-handled were once *de rigeur* features in an umbrella on the commuter bridges

titanium

but this has been superseded by the sponsored golf umbrella which allows a modicum of self expression while connoting 'team player' at a glance. It also brings a little of the weekend into the weekday; you can shelter beneath the suburban while the chaos of the urban rages around you. Familiar damp wafts of golf clubs, fairways and mid-range Rovers soothing your rabid brain.

UMBRELLA SHOP James Smith and Son, Hazelwood House, 53 New Oxford Street, London WC1A 1BL.[45]

BAG Gone are the days of compulsory leather briefcase or attaché. Some of the younger and camper City-bound venturers wear the diagonally slung wide-strapped Urban Excitement rucksack. Others still have adopted the record bag (too late by other gauges of cultural intensity).

There are advantages in carrying the traditional, more structured bag: as the unspeaking hordes battle for leg room and pathway position, a sharp nudge with the metal corner-reinforcement can do wonders. With eyes fixed firmly on the horizon, no one will suspect you of your crime. But you will have been given satisfaction all the same.

Women could adopt the perennial Kelly Bag to inflict a similar range of damage to their fellow travellers.

DANGER OF THEFT Carry valuable bags, computer cases or handbags on the inside of the flow of pedestrian traffic, towards a wall or row of parked cars. This offers less of an opportunity to a passer-by to snatch your bag and flee.

However, in London underground tunnels, carrying a bag in this way can be a problem. Where the pedestrian flow is directed to 'keep left' and as most walkers will be right handed, they will be forced to carry the bag in the weaker left hand. Some exercising and strengthening of the wrist and hand may be necessary to achieve the required grip in such a situation.

SHOES One of the most disappointing things about the City commuter is the tawdry and unimaginative selection of shoes that they have adopted.

Men are especially prone to old or cheap shoes, with very little regard for the traditional brogue or Oxford. Learning from our cousins across the Atlantic, women sometimes wear sensible training shoes for the sprint across the river, changing into more officey heels when at work. Men do this very rarely.

SUITS Grey. Rank is determined by grade of 'classic'. The upper reaches wearing classic waisted and vented three buttons over cut-away-collar shirt. Over-styled clothing marks the lower echelons of City worker; wide shoulders on suit or overcoat should be avoided. Similarly low-slung double-breasted jackets are a no-no.

HAIR Styles will generally be behind the times in City workers. Male middle management favour 1980s styles: shorter at the back, sweeping fringes, while younger guns detourn 'gay' styling with the gelled Tintin cowlick.

walking against the flow

Those massed against you are a special breed: brains boiled from standing for two hours on overcrowded trains; minds numbed through reciting timetables in their sleep: 'If I get up at 6.13, I can catch the 7.06 which gets me in at 8.43; unless it's late and then I'll get the late running 6.54.'

The choice is yours: match their crazed bullishness or use it to your advantage.

Test of nerve: rules of engagement
1 Find middle of pavement.
2 Adopt contraflow position, 'head-on' into the oncoming crowd.
3 Begin to walk against the flow.
4 Hold your line.
5 Keep looking straight ahead, making no eye-contact.
6 Force oncomers to move out of your way through your presence only.

How far can you get across the bridge?
Mark your progress in some way, with a chalked line for example.
Hold competitions with your friends to see how well they can do.
Variations: wear different clothing; walk with a partner; walk laterally, from edge to edge, perpendicular to the flow.

A NOTE TO VISITORS Try not to confuse London Bridge [D7 62] (the one with the miserable commuters) with Tower Bridge [F1 79] (the one in the brochure with the two gothic towers). It's easily done.

up and down

escalators

'Down escalators are one of the greatest inventions ever'
Bill Drummond, 45 (Little Brown 2000)

On London's underground system, you will find your ability to walk skilfully to be a great advantage. Visitors will wonder why standing two-abreast gets them hard stares and sore elbows. They are unaware of the rule of the escalator: 'keep right'.

On approaching the escalator, going either up or down, walkers will sort themselves into two subsets: 'left walkers' and 'right walkers'. The 'right walker' will be travelling at a a relatively low velocity and will be decelerating. On hitting the escalator, they will join the queue and come to rest on the first available step. They often adopt an attitude that is 'square on' to the step, relaxing on to the right handrail. A popular but advanced stance is characterised by the feet being on two steps with body-weight over one hip. Tourists and other slow walkers will be filtered into this subset.

The 'left walker' will be accelerating into an outside position, walking or running in pursuit of train or exit. 'Left walkers' are usually familiar with the tube, being workers or residents. Sometimes a visitor will switch from 'right' to 'left' after observing the etiquette on several journeys. This transition is worth the risk as it dramatically decreases the time taken underground.

A 'left walker' must operate in a reduced step-area when the right is occupied by a relaxed 'right walker'. 'Left walking' is unnecessary when the right of the step is unoccupied. A 'right walker' may step into the left and continue on their way as a 'left walker' only after looking back to check for overtaking pedestrian traffic. Once in the left, ascent or descent speed must equal that of existing 'left walkers'. If the strain gets too much, cut back to the right at the first opportunity afforded by free step-space.

travolators

Travolators, a rarity in London, can be installed either at an incline or on the horizontal. Some versions even have safety features such as a specially tapered handrail entry box. Examples can be found in London at Bank Underground Station [D6 62] where the 300-foot travolator links 'The Drain' or Waterloo and City Line to connecting lines. It has a gradient of 8 degrees. London Heathrow's terminals contain some good examples of the city's horizontal installations.

SIMPLE RULES FOR USING TRAVOLATORS

Take a long approach – this allows the walker time to adjust to movement of the travolator in relation to pavement.

Don't try to beat it – travolators are always installed for a good reason; it's further to walk than it first appears.

Keep right – as with escalators, this rule runs contrary to the London Transport signage.

Never look sideways – this upsets balance in the event of having jetlag, especially on exit from the travolator.

THE OUTSIDE Fight for and keep hold of the 'outside track' in these situations: spiral stairways; pavements; escalators.

spiral stairways

When the lifts are out of order in department stores and tube stations, or if you just want to keep fit on the cheap, try taking the stairs. In underground stations, the stairs will invariably be of a spiral constriction, the one obvious exception being the awkwardly spaced sloping stairs of 'The Drain'.

Spiral stairs can lead clockwise or anticlockwise. As those who follow the noble art of horse racing will know, whether a track runs to the left or right will determine the outcome of many a race. Comparable to the racehorse, the walker will have her/his own preference and should attempt speed descents on unfavoured tracks only after much practice.

The following is meant as advice to those who prize safety over bravado and whose main objective in life is to descend another stairway on another day:

> Spiral staircases: examples
> - Heal's [G5 61], Tottenham Court Road. Back of the shop to ground, first and second floors
> - Old Street Tube Station [D4 62]
> - Greenwich Foot Tunnel entrances [E5 80]
> - South Bank Centre [K1 77]: entrance from south, stairs to upper concourses and Hungerford Bridge.

DESCENDING THE STAIRCASE Ascent of the spiral stairway is a matter of stamina and strength and deserves little attention. Conversely, descent is by far the greater challenge to the walker, a test of nerve as well as of physical prowess.

The useful walking area of a spiral stairway will tend to be narrow, towards the outside edge of the steps. Keeping to this 'outside track' is necessary so as to have maximum step width to play with. It is the most comfortable track to take. It is possible to take the inside, but leave this to Flash Harries wanting to overtake, and to those who don't mind the risk of damage to ankle ligaments.

> Remember: the outside track lets you see ahead into oncoming traffic, something denied to you as you sprint in tiny Ali-shuffle steps down the inside. Using the outside contributes to a reduction in accident and injury.

As with road traffic, it is the descendee's responsibility to change course on meeting with an ascendee.

SPIRAL STAIR TECHNIQUES You can quickly be fooled into thinking that you have understood and mastered the step height, depth and frequency. Be aware of your feet at every step. Don't look down or back.

STAIRS: LOOK FOR THE SIGNS In tube stations, you will often be informed of the number of steps that lie ahead. You will soon get a feel for how far 100 steps actually is. Try Old Street or Kennington stations on the Northern Line for practice.

Note to neophytes: do not attempt stairs-to-exit at Hampstead as it is the deepest station on the London Underground, some 58.5 metres (192 feet) below ground level.[46]

STEPS AND GEOLOGY From the number of stairs, and hence the depth of the station, you will be able to work out the geological terrain of London, the deeper stations being on the north side of the Thames.

pavements and surfaces

The pavements that you walk will vary greatly in dimension, finish and material. They should be, each and every one of them in turn, the walker's best friend, partner, and lover. Get to know and understand the surfaces on which you walk and you will be repaid greatly. Secrets will be retold and great truths revealed.

ANATOMY OF A TYPICAL PAVEMENT According to A J McCormack and Son in their comprehensive online resource, 'A Guide to UK Paving Materials and Methods', these are the component layers and materials that constitute a typical pavement:[47]

sub-grades: the existing ground, cleared of any organic material

sub-bases: the load-bearing layer, usually constructed from 'crushed and graded stone'

bedding layer: usually of coarse grit sand, with low clay content and good drainage properties

paving layer: 'The final hard surface of the paving. This may be concrete or clay blocks, pre-cast concrete flags, natural stone or any other form of paving'.

PAVING MATERIALS

Natural materials:

gravel – small rounded or angular pebbles, size range: 3mm to 18mm

cobbles, setts – natural stone blocks, size range: 50mm x 50mm x

50mm to 350mm x 200mm x 250mm
York stone – flat slabs of natural stone, a low maintenance 'paving of character'
duckstones – large pebbles.

Manufactured materials:
concrete flags/slabs – precast slabs of concrete
concrete patio flags
decorative flags – three common types: textured, decorative, riven
concrete block paving
concrete brick – three common types: modern rectangular, olde worlde block, shaped blocks. ('THE growth area in paving over the last 10 years' (McCormack)
clay brick paving
clay bricks
pattern imprinted concrete
coloured concrete
plain concrete hardstanding
plain concrete
Tarmac
tar-coated aggregates
resin-bonded aggregates
small pebbles

FLAGS AND SLABS As London is in the south of England, the final layer of pavement that you walk on will be referred to as a 'slab', rather than 'flag' as it would be called in other parts of the UK.

Checklist for the prevention of slip and trip hazards:
Is each suitable for the environment where used?
Is each surface for the work activity (eg resistance to chemicals,

oil, grease, hot substances)?

Is each surface suitable for the type and amount of traffic?

Is each surface in good condition and free from damage or unevenness which could cause hazards?

Are any changes in level of surfaces (small steps, slopes etc) liable to be unnoticed due to inadequate lighting?

Are all staircases fitted with handrails and, where appropriate, anti-slip tread in good condition?

From the TUC's *One Stop Safety & Health Shop for Trade Unionists*

surface detail and footwear

The thinner the sole of your shoes, the more detail you will be able to feel underfoot. It follows that rich ladies and poor children will be those to acquire the most knowledge of the flaws and quirks of London's pathways.

SAME PLACE, DIFFERENT SHOES In research and testing for this book, I walked in both Clarks Wallabee shoes and Merrell all-terrain slip-ons to experience a range of sensations, support, grip and the like under very similar pathing circumstances. The Wallabees' crepe sole was best suited to walks of less distance in mixed shopping and walking situations. They do, however, allow the transmission of detailed information regarding pavement, road conditions and construction to the foot. The Merrells, while being unparalleled in their comfort over long distance and in uneven terrain, conveyed very little detail to the wearer. The air-cushioned sole with high treading gives superb handling but turns London's streets into an undifferentiated surface, free of inflexion, rhythm or tension.

Of course the entire gamut of shoe soles cannot be expe-

Clarks

rienced by one person in a lifetime as short as that imposed upon humankind. But from interviews conducted with the wearers of other types of shoes, it is possible to build a picture of a population stratified by sole thickness and heel height; each aware to differing degrees of the implication of conditions underfoot for their experience of London.

PROBLEM SURFACES FOR HIGH HEELS:
    marble
    carpet
    cobbles
    cracked paving stones
    escalator slats
    drain covers
    cellar grilles
    glass and highly glazed floor tiles
    soft Tarmac.

high heels
According to 22-year-old Morgana, political science student from Trieste, Italy: 'Stiletto heels are a powerful tool in the service of our femininity, but we must never forget that this same tool can quickly become a disadvantage'. Her comprehensive online guide to 'how walking becomes graceful and feminine' can prove useful should you wish to tackle London's thoroughfares in anything from $2^3/_4$ inch to $5^1/_2$ inch heels (up to $7^1/_2$ inches when matched with 4-inch platforms).[48]

Bear in mind that Italians measure the height of heels differently to the way it is done in both Britain and the USA, widely underestimating the altitude by up to 20 per cent, but Morgana insists that anything over $5^1/_2$ inches seriously

just walk normal

compromises the possible articulation of the ankle. Any heel advertising a height beyond this will be aided by a platform sole of some kind, if it is intended for any sort of practical walking purpose.

> Heel height – the vertical distance from the center of the top-piece where it contacts the ground to the seat of the shoe. There is, however, much difference of opinion as to how this measurement should be taken, because of differences of seat angle with the horizontal and top-piece location in a fore and aft sense.
> The above definition assumes that the center of the top-piece is vertically below the center of pressure of the weight-bearing protuberance of the lower surface of the heel bone. In practice the height is most commonly measured at the back of the heel, vertically upward from ground surface to seat.[49]

HIGH-HEEL TECHNIQUE Cross-sectional and longitudinal balancing are the keys to stability. A mistake commonly made is to bend the knees, splay the legs or do the 'actress or model' walk, as if aiming either foot at an imaginary straight line, 'sashaying' in some sense. The 'correct position of your legs should not be that very different from normal'. This will come to you over time, after the initial bouts of self-consciousness and lateral wobble. It is also recommended that newcomers to this form of footwear graduate to the highest levels in 'small doses'; starting out at up to 3 inches, progressing up to 4 inches on the first upgrade. From there you're on your own.

Regular exercises, such as walking around the house or flat on the balls of your feet for ten minutes per day are said to help no end.

Heel phase 1-3

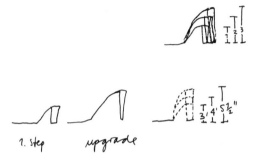

T   T
2   3
1   1

1. step   upgrade

T   T   T
3   4   5 ½"
1   1

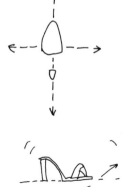

WHO TO BUY Manolo Blahnik, Old Church Street, SW3 [B5 76]. Famed internationally for his mules, he has been quoted as saying, 'If you're small, do not wear very high heels. I think it's the wrong proportion. If you're small, wear small heels. If you try to be high, it's wrong.'

Kurt Geiger, New Bond Street, W1 [F7 61] and department stores

Sacha, Foubert's Place, W1 [G6 61] for very high heels

Jimmy Choo, big in Hollywood, teamed with a Daniel Swarovski handbag.

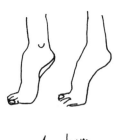

at home

surviving weather conditions

Although some have attributed great powers of prescience to London's weather (Sinclair 1997: p89), it presents little in the way of extremes to the London walker. However, a real hazard is presented through its contrast with climate-control systems in built environments.

Travelling on tube trains or walking into some office spaces, dramatic differences of temperature and humidity will present a forceful challenge.

weather conditions

Be prepared for the worst. Keen as you might be to check exterior weather conditions from the ludicrously animated weather zombies on local BBC television news, other services such as the Weather Underground[50] are useful, as are the web-cams at http://www.webviews.co.uk/london/ or http://www.mbridge.ft.com/blankhi.html#.

hot weather

For three months of the year London can be a sticky and sweaty experience. Unlike the inhabitants of some other European cities, Londoners don't take flight from the city *en masse* in high summer. Cut-off suits have been the biggest concession made to the heat of June, July and August. Otherwise, London sits it out with little or no air-conditioning in private dwellings and maybe some corporate chilled-water dispensers at work.

OVERHEATING The US Government's Centers for Disease Control and Prevention recommend the following for those overtaken by extreme heat: cool, non-alcoholic beverages; rest; cool shower, bath, or sponge bath; an air-conditioned environment; lightweight clothing.

WEIGHT OF CLOTHING As a general rule, wear less and wear lighter when in London than anywhere else in Britain.

BLAST OF A/C When you can't stand the heat as you walk, head for one of the larger retail chains or department stores and linger in the climate-controlled shopping environment just long enough to cool off, calm down and continue on your way. This is best effected if you are already sweaty as the evaporation that will occur acts to lower the body's temperature.

COOL SHOWER If you do not sweat at a high enough rate, carry a small atomiser-spray containing a mixture of water and aloe vera to spray the face and neck when walking in heat.

cold weather

The Union of Shop Distributive and Allied Workers (USDAW) insists in *Heat Stress at Work* that 13 degrees C is the minimum temperature for those whose work involves physical activity.[51] But what happens when we have to walk under conditions that contravene such regulations?

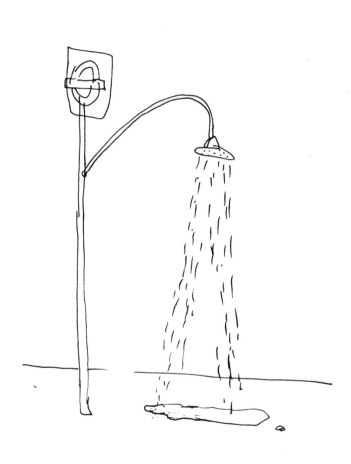

WIND CHILL As a living, breathing walker, metabolising, moving muscles and thereby generating heat, you will experience the phenomenon of wind chill when walking in cold and windy conditions.

Wind chill serves to make the walker feel colder than the actual air temperature: perspiration emitted by the body evaporates, cooling the body faster than it can heat itself by for example, shivering or some other muscle movement.

> Formula for calculating wind chill factor
> $WC = 0.0817(3.71S-0.5 + 5.81 -0.25v)(T - 91.4) + 91.4$
> Where WC is the wind chill, S is the wind speed in miles per hour and T is the temperature in degrees Fahrenheit.

WALKING IN COLD WEATHER Cold weather presents a serious challenge: how to dress in an appropriate way while avoiding hypothermia and frostbite. Check the following well-meant advice from the US Government's Centers for Disease Control and Prevention. It soon turns sour when you realise the full impact it would have on your sartorial state:

- a scarf or knit mask to cover face and mouth
- sleeves that are snug at the wrist
- mittens (they are warmer than gloves)
- water-resistant coat and shoes
- several layers of loose-fitting clothing.

Following this advice, walkers would be warm but shamed into staying indoors, defeating the whole exercise.

Far better to keep your present wardrobe intact, tailored as it is to fit your particular social and cultural milieu, and seek what the city can do for you to help you keep warm.

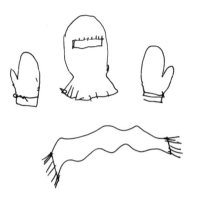

Lost mittens:

Nr. 1   Nr. 2   Nr. 3   Nr. 4

Although London in the winter months can be bleak and unforgiving, even the coldest places can offer you warmth when you least expect it. The wearing of mittens will remain someone else's burden.

WARMTH FOR FREE Walking in winter through the City of London at night or weekends, you see very few pedestrians braving the icy wind blasting through the narrow streets. But thanks to the generosity of the financial-services industry, there are some 'hot-spots' to be found, where the public can bathe in the glorious gusts of warm air tumbling from lobby and underground car park.

1 'Barclay's Corner' [D7 68], where Gracechurch Street meets Lombard Street, has a welcoming heated grille in the pavement outside the bank itself. Recommended for warming the feet only: the hot air does not rise far, being whisked away by the turbulent colder air which circulates on this corner.
2 The windows opposite the NatWest tower in Old Broad Street [E6 62] and the access doors around the corner in Winchester Street waft very warm air towards the pavement at night. Warm enough to feel on your knees as you walk past. Highly recommended for lifting both general body temperature and emotional state.
3 South of Mansion House towards Cannon Street Station in Walbrook [D7 62] there is a service entrance to an office block on the left that blasts hot air on to the street. Hotter even than the Barclay's Corner updraft.
4 A very intense heat source can be found at the site of road repair or construction work: hot Tarmac raises the ambient temperature considerably and also gives a very

quick blast of heat to the soles of the feet when briefly walked upon. Not recommended for those wearing shoes whose soles have a low melting point; crepe is particularly prone to disintegration. Leather is more robust under these conditions.

5 Jonathan Routh makes the further suggestion in his *Weekend Guide* (Routh 1969: p104): that it is possible to find heat in the tropical bird house at London Zoo [E2 60] during the day. This recommendation can also be extended to the tropical houses at Kew Gardens [E2 89].

COLD SPOTS It's an icy westerly that swirls around Centre Point [H6 61] on to the north side of New Oxford Street.

THE URBAN HEAT ISLAND The difference in temperature between the West End and Bow, a district on the marshes out in the east, can be striking. The central areas can be described as a potential 'urban heat island' due to the differences between its energy gains and losses.

It is characterised by:

- increased waste heat from buildings, vehicles and people. This can be equal to up to one third of the heat energy provided by the Sun
- less cooling by evaporation
- being constructed from good conductors such as brick, asphalt and concrete that warm the surrounding air
- tall buildings which trap infrared and solar energy in the canyons between them
- increase in precipitation, fog and cloudiness as a result of thermal circulation.

This phenomenon is negated when winds are more than 20mph as cooler rural air mixes with and decreases the warmth in the urban area.[51]

wet

It is when out in the wet that you are most likely to be tempted from your commitment to walking. You may find yourself dreaming of bed and of driving a large, warm, dry car.

If you find yourself in the rain, avoiding the tidal waves pushed from puddles and gutter run-offs by safe-and-warm drivers, collar of coat hitched up, feet soaking and eyes full of slurried street grit, you know you're not walking for leisure or pleasure. It's at times like these that the body locks down and shuts off all unnecessary functions, such as senses of humour or humanity. It's you against the elements and all other obstacles thrown at you: fight or flight the only choices. Your aim will be clear: get through this with least fuss.

PUDDLES In heavy rain, when surface water gathers at the roadside, be sure to walk against the flow of road traffic. This will give you advance warning of puddles and their proximity to oncoming vehicles. With practice, it is possible to judge when to pass large areas of surface water without getting soaked to the skin. Learn how to adjust your speed against that of the coming road traffic and to pass by in the gaps between the flow of malevolent drivers slamming into puddles.

THE DANGER OF OTHER PEOPLE'S UMBRELLAS Depending on

your height, you will experience the use of umbrellas in different ways. People of less than average height – less than 5 feet 4 inches (163 cm) – will experience less rainfall when walking among umbrella users. They are able to move freely below the canopy and can take full advantage of the benefits of other people's umbrellas. Possible disadvantages include increased susceptibility to rain run-off which, in areas of high-density umbrella use or where erratic movement is experienced, can prove unpredictable and devastating to levels of personal comfort.

Taller than average walkers will not benefit from the use of umbrellas by others. The head and eye areas will be uncomfortably close to the ends of whirling umbrella spokes which, if not causing actual damage, will bring on irritability in many.

Taller walkers should also be aware of the 6-foot ceiling on the tunnel at Lazenby Court, the thoroughfare between Garrick Street and Floral Street which passes next to the Lamb & Flag pub.

UNDERCOVER IN OXFORD STREET A widely known and utilised technique for staying dry when journeying down Oxford Street works equally well when searching for shade. The long canopies which run outside department stores are a remarkable asset to the pedestrian. Supposedly constructed to shelter the window shopper and reduce glare and fade-inducing direct sunlight on the window displays, they provide an indoors–outdoors; a luxury. And it's free.

The route
Direction: east to west (can be reversed).
Start on the north side of Oxford Street at Oxford Circus, Hennes

pass through towards BHS; through to John Lewis; through to Debenhams; through to Selfridges. You will now be at Orchard Street, at the south end of Baker Street, having traversed the main shopping area of Oxford Street.

OBSERVATIONS ON IN-STORE SHORTCUTTING When you are walking through a shop you will be affected by several factors:

- Perimeter heating: a blast of hot or cold air at the entrance to a shop can have dramatic effects on your progress. Experiencing relative extremes of hot or cold can force a break of stride, slowing you enough to be vulnerable to impulse purchase. Keep moving at all costs

- store layout: some stores are aware of the practice of in-store shortcutting and will place obstacles in your way. Wise to the needs of the urban walker, you will find snack foodstuffs used tactically. More strategic use of obstacles can be seen in Selfridges, where all routes lead inward, towards the heart of the retail machine

- the density of low-velocity shoppers: A high density will act as resistance to the speed and direction of movement

- the efficacy of store security: They seem suspicious of everyone, even legitimate purchasers. You have paid once, but what else will you cram into that bag unnoticed? On Saturdays security guards become 'itchy', faced by hordes of marauding teens from the outer districts, 'steaming' into clothes shops on the trail of Moschino or Versace or whatever Missy Elliot or Mary J is wearing on MTV. As a walker, a shortcutter, you should have no fear of these people. Remember,

shop staff themselves are the biggest embezzellers of all.
They'll give the guards all that they're looking for ...

SHADOW WALK

A game for at least two players, one of whom must be an in-store
security guard.

Player 1 should behave in a 'normal' manner in a retail environment: browsing, checking sizes, quality of fabric, finish and price.

Player 2, preferably wearing a peaked, paramilitary-style cap,
should interpret all behaviour as suspicious and act accordingly,
closely following player 1.

Player 2 should make no attempt at subtlety.

Player 1 should remain in the retail environment for as long as possible, keeping player 2's attention throughout, tempting him/her to
follow and do the 'shadow walk'.

The winner is the player who catches the other looking directly at
them.

timing

You're free from the constraints of work. There'll be no clock watching. Time is your own. Your body is free to determine the things you do; how far you walk; where; when. Why use clock time? Given that London is the capital of time, being drilled through by the Prime Meridian, you would expect not to be able to escape its influence. But be determined and it can be done.

human metabolism

BE AWARE OF YOUR BODY. BE AWARE OF ITS DEMANDS.

There are times when the harmonious coupling of mind and body is tested to the limit; when the finely tuned and carefully balanced machine of which you understand yourself to be composed just lets you down. The body gets a grip on you, an upper hand, pulls a half-nelson on your brain and slams it to the floor. Sugar levels plummet faster than a BASE jumper with an amnesiac bag-packer and you're in need of instant refuelling. Time to eat.

This can be a useful way of structuring walks, as it has always been. For example, travel by horse in Britain used to be assisted by a network of taverns and coach houses which served refreshments at distances from London which show some correspondence between hunger, distance and time.

BODY'S DEMANDS Here are some ideas for using the body's demand for food to your walking-advantage:

1 Eat nothing while walking. Keep walking until you faint. Be sure to note your start and finish points when you regain consciousness.
2 Carry a large amount of food, as much as you can carry, and eat constantly as you walk. See how far you get.
3 Carry lots of money and stop at a shop to buy one item of food. Walk on until the item is finished. Stop at the next shop and continue the process until you run out of money.
4 Begin walking and be aware of the demands that your body makes of you. Stop for food and drink whenever necessary and make a record of the tension between clock time and body time.

KNOWING WHEN TO EAT Learn to identify patterns in your behaviour and to know what is your 'normal' condition. Maybe you'll experience mood swings. If the mood swings are in an 'upward' direction from your normally depressed state, then there's nothing I can recommend to you. It can't be that bad. But if you're normally a happy-go-lucky character with a spring in your step and a smirk on your face, your mood could swing down, deeper and down. In 1996, the American Diabetes Association identified 'behavioural changes as primary features of a low blood glucose' in children rather than adults. So if you're a sufferer of food-related mood swings and the main symptom is being a crabby git, then maybe you're younger than you look.

LOW BLOOD SUGAR Unless you already have some experience

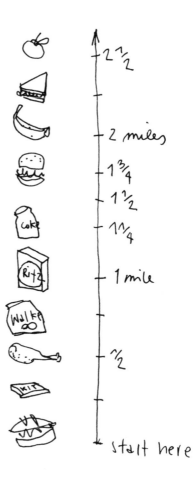

2½

2 miles

1¾

1½

1¼

1 mile

½

coke

Ritz

Walke

KIT

start here

of the various forms of hypoglycaemia, these are the symptoms of low blood sugar to watch-out for:

- Fatigue: and this means real fatigue. I take it that you're active enough if you've bought this book, so you'll know what it's like to be fit and healthy. And what it's like to be tired.
- General discomfort, uneasiness, or ill-feeling (malaise): a great proportion of London is run on small wages and long hours or huge wages and long hours, on short contracts and in a competitive environment. This is the general condition under which most people who live here operate.
- Nervousness: London's a big city and can seen daunting if it's your first time out. Don't mistake environmentally instigated nervousness for food-induced nervousness.
- Irritability: the crowds you'll face when shopping in the West End or the smug faces you'll see while stalking Clerkenwell will give you the hump, no doubt. Try as best you can to distinguish between the causes of your irritability, whether it is internal or external.
- Trembling and headache: both are as likely to be brought about by consuming large amounts of alcoholic beverages. Again, nothing to do with genuine food-related 'low blood sugar'.
- Hunger: a true hypoglycaemic may be so confused (see below) as to totally misunderstand the signs of hunger. If you've ever felt your guts flip when passing a chip shop, you'll know everything's in working order. This is an easy test to undertake – though finding a half-decent chippy in Greater London is tougher than you'd think. If from Yorkshire, you will face extreme disappointment

in the outcome of this quest.

- Sweats: hot sweat? Cold sweat? When it's time to change your shirt, it's either a Tuesday or you've got one of the symptoms, bad.
- Rapid heart rate: the average human heart rate is 70 bpm. How's yours?
- Blurry or double vision: they charge for eye tests in the UK now. It all used to be free. So if your eyes aren't what they were but you can't stand paying to have them corrected, you might well experience this symptom anyway. But if you can read this, chances are you're OK.
- Confusion: it can happen. A drop in 'blood sugar' can negate even the supreme confidence that you'll have through digesting the contents of this book. Being bewildered and in public in London is hazardous; get some food in you ASAP, before the next meal you get is intravenous and comes courtesy of the National Health Service.
- Convulsions: stop reading. Go home. Get help.
- Coma: it's been nice knowing you.

And the information provided herein should not be used for diagnosis or treatment of any medical condition. A general practitioner should be consulted for diagnosis and treatment of any and all medical conditions.

Don't take my word for it: check the online resources for hypoglycaemia[52] for a thorough description of causes, symptoms and diagnosis, treatments, alternative care and self care and prevention.

BURN CALORIES LIKE CRAZY
Walking at three miles per hour burns about 60–80 calories per mile.

CALORIFIC VALUES OF MACRONUTRIENTS:
4 kilocalories per gram of carbohydrate
4 kilocalories per gram of protein
9 kilocalories per gram of fat
7 kilocalories per gram of alcohol

CALORIFIC VALUES OF SPECIFIC CAKES AND PASTRIES[53]

Item and weight) (grams)	Calorific value (kilocalories)
Plain (60g)	390
Fruit (60g)	355
Sponge (60g)	465
Eclair (50g)	375
Jam tart (35g)	385
Lemon meringue (120g)	325
Doughnut (40g)	350
Custard tart (120g)	285

FAVOURITE CAKE AND PASTRY OUTLETS Rest up at Maison Berteaux, 28 Greek Street, W1 [H6 61] or The Evering Bakery, Brick Lane, E1 [F4 63].

the business of walking

Catching the bus, walking to the shops to buy something before it shuts or they run out, walking to a cash-point machine, walking to work; these are all ways in which walking is bounded and determined by accurate readings of clock time. You daren't be late and you wouldn't want to be anyhow. There are occasions when events determine your relationship to time. Here are some ways to keep in step with the world as it turns: 'time's money' ...

people
London can be a lonely place and when you regularly see a face you recognise you can feel, just for an instant, that you're part of 'village London' a tight-knit community that you knew existed somewhere but you couldn't ever get to experience first hand. Those sociological studies of the East End, Mr Wilmot and Mr Young's famous study of 'kinship', as they so anachronistically called the network of 'friends and family' that British Telecom more accurately describes, fuelled a folk history of tight familial bonding, sympathies across generations and a tendency towards the tribal. Try as you might, if you're wearing the wrong haircut and paid full whack for your Reeboks, you're not likely to get close to the Cockney and her social milieu.

nautical timepieces
Western navigation techniques rely on knowing the time. In the 1700s John Harrison consolidated the British obsession with knowing exactly where you stand when he invented a means of transporting time over distance, thereby making it possible to determine longitude. His scientific breakthrough has generated a flurry of media spin-offs in recent times, most spectacularly from the BBC, who chose the reassuring voice-over tones of Tim Piggot-Smith, the man so often associated with film and TV's fawning to other Great British Men at Great British Moments (Winston Churchill, Francis Crick, John Major) in their tangentially titled *Longitude* of 1997.[54]

But to see his work in the flesh, go to the exhibition of his chronometers at the Greenwich (formerly Greenwich Magnetic) Observatory [F7 81].

time and space

You could measure time by the distance covered while travelling, or how long it might take to perform a task. In the Ottoman empire, time was measured by how far a man and horse could ride. The inhabitants of the Ottoman Empire also had a different idea of how much an hour was. The 'oriental' concept was determined by the technical development of the country. In the Ottoman empire the travelling Englishman was thrown back into an age where no railways or coaches existed. Physical fatigue of horse and rider determined travelling distances.

Time and space were difficult to separate in Turkey because the space stretches were measured by the time it took a man to ride through them, the pace being that of a man on a long journey:

> Where the ground is good, and no hills intervene, as on the Dobrudja, 'an hour' would represent a little over four miles, but in the mountainous districts not more than three, and it will sometimes happen that when there are two roads both going to the same place, the longest by mileage will be much the shortest by hours. (Barkley, Bulgaria, 93–4.)'
> Dora Panayotova[55]

time and product

Some people measure time in cigarettes – the duration taken from lighting to extinguishing or from buying to finishing a packet. In times when smoking was more popular than it is now, many people could understand that 'your house is three ciggies from mine'. Now that smoking is less common – even banned in many places – you'll be more likely to say that 'your house is one bacon double cheeseburger and regular fries away from mine'. Evidence of this is easy to spot: if you ever buy a take-away product, become aware of when you finish it and when you either dump the wrapper or look for a bin.

You will find that thousands have been there before you and take-out debris will be all around. You are looking at one measure of time according to 'take-away time'. Burger products are best for timing a walk in this way. The box that is given to you as brand identification and reinforcement for the food product also acts as a receptacle for serviette and lettuce shards and, more importantly, stops mayo, ketchup and fat dribbling down your shirt. Given these qualities, it is a product that persists for as long as it takes you to eat your meal and not a moment longer. It is at this point that the box becomes surplus to requirements and must be discarded.

Wrapper-drop is easy to master if you are of a generation born too late to experience Roy Hudd leaping over park benches, daring you to become a litter lout for fear of turning out like him – doomed to the outer reaches of BBC Radio 2 and mid-afternoon ITV sofa-quizzes.

You can try this even with popular chocolate bars. The introduction of the Jumbo KitKat saw extended ripples of plastic-paper emanate from corner shops everywhere, marking the limit of existence for the new-fangled bar; the moment of complete ingestion and wrapper-drop.

RECEIPTS Forgotten your watch? Too shy to ask a passer-by?

441/443,BRIXTON ROAD,BRIXTON
TELEPHONE 0171-737-4566

```
    5 Onion Bagels          £
    5 Onion Bagels          0.95
** MULTIBUY **              0.95
SUBTOTAL                    0.95-D
ITEM DISCOUNT               1.90
SUBTOTAL                    0.95-D
    CASH                    0.95 *
    CHANGE                  1.00
    NO OF ITEMS 2           0.05
```

ICELAND SPECIAL OFFERS HAS REDUCED
    YOUR SHOPPING BILL BY £0.95

31.05.00 20:28 9129   20 J 162

ICELAND VAT NUMBER 682 3453 26
THANK YOU FOR SHOPPING WITH US

No need to worry: find a shop with an electronic till and make a purchase. The time and date will be printed at the foot of your receipt.

moving

NUMBER OF WALKERS When walking accompanied by others, your walking style may change markedly. Your party may show signs of self-organisation or you may adopt or have imposed upon you a party 'leader'.

FOLLOWING If you are walking alone but wish to experience some of the sensations of walking with others, there are several things to try: following an individual and following a crowd.

DOUBLE OR QUITS

New Yorker Paul Auster, in his novel *Leviathan* of 1992, based the life of Maria on that of artist and Parisienne Sophie Calle. From a brief episode grounded in fact, 'on pages 60 to 67 of his book' (Calle, 1999) Maria lives on in the rest of the novel as fiction.

Calle continues to pursue this idea of the fictive double:

'Since *Leviathan*, Auster has taken me as a subject, I imagined swapping roles and taking him as the author of my actions. I asked him to invent a fictive character which I would attempt to resemble. I was, in effect, inviting Paul Auster to do what he wanted with me, for a period of up to a year at most. Auster objected that he did not want to take responsibility for what might happen when I acted out the script he had created for me. He preferred to send me "Personal instructions for S.C. On How to Improve Life in New York City (Because she asked)". I followed his directives. This project is entitled Gotham Handbook.' (Calle, 1999)

Auster's instructions can be paraphrased as:

1 Smile when least expected.
2 Talk to strangers – give flattering comments.
3 Give sandwiches and ciggies to beggars and homeless people.
4 Cultivate a spot – make one location in the city your own. 'Beautify it'. Watch it for one hour at the same time everyday.
5 If in doubt, talk about the weather.

Through the 'Gotham Handbook' Calle texually and photographically records her sandwiches, her spot and her strangers. Her artwork is played-out on the street; using other peoples' movements to determine her walking behaviour: where she will walk, when, and in what guise.

Reversing this formula, it is possible to extend the 'double game' that she plays. Her artwork can be used to structure your life and your walking.

For example, track her movements in *Frieze*, *Art Monthly*, *Flash Art* and other specialist art publications, or on websites. Check with airlines and hotels. Wear disguises. Leave notes in hotels, in drawers, in Venice, in bed …

Calle is less than ubiquitous however, and it may be an idea to apply these techniques to those who crop-up with greater regularity in listings pages; or pick artists according to alphabetical order and walk to their exhibitions. This will soon give you a specialist knowledge of E1, E2 and E3 or SW1, N1 and W1 if you're lucky.

WHAT'S THE TIME MR WOLF? This childhood game is an ideal device to use when following someone. Most suited to generating confrontational walks.

Description and rules
This is a game played in childhood but soon dropped once players

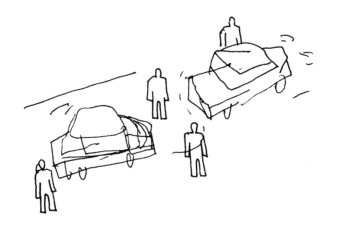

playing Mr. Wolf on the Street

realise that it's not a real wolf that's being sneaked up on.

The rules of the game, which can be played anywhere and with anyone, are simple:

• The 'wolf' must be walking away from you.
• You have to follow them.
• They turn round.
• If you're still moving and they see you you're 'out'.
• Get close enough to touch them and they're 'out': you win and you get to be the wolf next go.

This is a great game to play with friends, and takes on another dynamic when played with strangers. Try walking along behind whoever it is in the conventional manner, trying to go unnoticed, or do things to attract attention but stop when they turn. Was it you making those noises? Was it you breathing down their necks? Hours or minutes of fun to be had, depending on local magistrates and tolerance levels.

The average time for someone to react to being watched is between 10 and 30 seconds.

STALKER When you want to walk but have no real reason and when you've got so much time on your hands, celebrities are useful as a structuring device. They can pad out an otherwise shapeless existence. They have too little time, too much money and all the right reasons to want to walk unobstructed to wherever they want to go. They'll be direct, focused and chaperoned or bodyguarded if they're of the top-flight variety.

The principle for using celebrities to help you walk is similar to that for the 'What's the time ...?' device detailed above. Following undetected is recommended, as forfeits can be costly and restraining orders detrimental to your walking pleasure.

It's worth bearing in mind that thanks to the high turn-over of feature-fodder in celeb mags such as *Hello!* and OK there are always new celebrities to help satisfy the enormous demand for structure in ordinary people's lives.

GROUP WALKING ISSUES Problems that will occur when group walking include:

- bunching
- heel treading
- slow decision-making and difficulty in steering
- poor judgement of width
- incorrect judgement of speed: you will achieve a slower speed when walking in a crowd than you might if walking alone.

SPEED OF MOVEMENT Some parts of London impose constraints on the pace at which you may walk. When in very crowded situations – Christmas shopping in the West End for example – you will have to adhere to the speed restrictions imposed by tired, visiting shoppers and their tired, reluctant families. Any attempt to confound them will frustrate both you and them.

Walking at slow speeds in fast-moving traffic, at rush hours for example, when large numbers of people make a short dash for freedom, you stand to be mown down, cajoled or mobbed, any or all of which you will deserve.

walkers, wanderers, night walkers, loiterers

walker – some people prefer walker to pedestrian (*q.v.*). It is short, descriptive of a variety of purposes, including recreation

and transportation. The word walker concentrates on the
humanity of people on foot, rather than the bureaucratic and
Latinate pedestrian.
International Pedestrian Lexicon

You are defined by the speed at which you walk. Walk
slowly in some of London's few red-light districts and you
will soon find yourself embarrassed or rich, depending on
how you play it. You will appear to be acting suspiciously if
at any time you contravene the norms of movement or pace
in any given area. The Broadgate office complex [E5 62], for
example, demands a very high throughput of bodies; anyone
with contradictory habits will immediately come under
scrutiny at the multiplexed security desks.

Dawdling becomes loitering when practised in certain
London public parks. Loitering in turn becomes cottaging
when practised in certain London public lavatories.

The walker, to remain a walker and to retain the dignity
of self-determination, should always be sensitive to the
demands of a changing environment. Be flexible, adaptable
and versatile and you have it made; nothing to worry about.

TAXI CRAWL There are no tubes running and you've missed
the bus home from the West End. When you can't face waiting any longer, you start to walk. You may be the worse for
wear in whatever way is currently making its way from the
style press to the Sunday supplements.

Keep a clear head and look out for one particular preda-
tor: the minicab driver is out there somewhere. And he's
looking for you.

IDENTIFYING THE MINICAB A minicab for private hire should,

by definition and by law, be unlike a taxi in either design or appearance. Invariably, they willingly comply with these stipulations, being more likely to be a ten-year-old Japanese saloon in red or white; a stark contrast to the ubiquitous FX4s, TX1s, Metrocabs or even the rare Asquith (only eleven licensed, August 1999).

ON BEING SOLICITED BY MINICABS Legally, minicabs should be booked through a licenced operator as they are not permitted to tout for business on the street. Evidence to the contrary can be found from late afternoon onwards at St Giles Circus [H6 61] (at the junction of Tottenham Court Road, Charing Cross Road and Oxford Street). Display signs of being in need of a cab, such as looking tired, lost or mashed, and they will seek you out. In the West End this will take the form of a direct oral request.

These advances can be ignored with reciprocal directness:

1 Just say no and keep walking.
2 Ignore the request altogether and keep walking.
3 Pretend to be a student looking for one of the English
   language schools above the shopfronts of the west end
   of Oxford Street, and keep walking.

In the city late at night, be vigilant for slow-moving oncoming vehicles. A flash of headlights from dipped to full will indicate that the car is an unmarked minicab. At first, you may mistake the flashes for the car's pitching and rolling over a rough road or 'sleeping policeman'; they will be subtle gestures but nevertheless this cab is touting for business. Action: unless unable to walk any further, ignore advances;

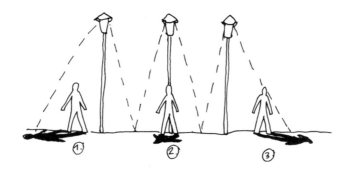

① when approaching street lights shadow behind
② when under → underneath
③ when overtake street light → shadow overtakes you

keep looking ahead and maintain an even stride, disguising all outward signs of drunkenness or any other frailty that could leave you vulnerable to other solicitors.

SHADOW WATCHING After dark, watch the play of shadows to check who is nearby.

1 Look ahead to junctions of roads or alleys for shadows cast in your path.
2 Look down to your immediate left and right for shadows cast from behind you. Your motion when walking will take you between street lights. As you near one, moving away from another, shadows will appear to duplicate; even your own shadow may seem to be overtaking you at times.

chronometers

PUBLIC TIMEPIECES You may be on your way to meet a loved one and you have the feeling that you're running late. You may need to catch the shops before they shut, or kill some time before they open. Whatever the purpose, you need to know what time it is. For those without the benefit of personal timepieces, here are some types and locations of public clocks and watches.

WATCH AND CLOCK SHOPS When in a hurry, or when not cash-rich, you can use clock shops to gauge the correct time. Scan a broad range of watch and clock faces; look for the time indicated on the majority of them; accept this average as being the correct time.

CHEAP WATCHES Many cheap end-of-line watches can be

found in the electronics shops on Tottenham Court Road [H5 61]. Be prepared for evasive and erratic customer-service techniques. Haggling is permitted on some items so don't show too much enthusiasm when browsing for bargains.

OFFICES Offices are full of clock watchers, so take a peek through the broken vertical blinds and search out the white plastic clockface with its tortuous red second hand heralding the freedom that lies ahead.

other people's watches

BY REQUEST It is still possible, in most parts of 'inner' London, to stop a passer-by and request the time from them. Where not to ask the time: Knightsbridge [C3 76]. Do not expect a reply to your request for the time here. In recent years, this area of London, with its high density of wealth, has been the target of Rolex thieves. Locals and travellers in this area are now extremely wary of both muggers or car-jackers who will release you from the burden of watch-ownership in seconds.

BY STEALTH People reading newspapers invariably wear watches. While reading their *Evening Standard* they will expose their watch as they raise their arms to position the paper correctly. The watch will appear upside-down but, with practice, it is possible to read a watchface from any angle.

PUBLIC CLOCKS Some public-minded citizens give you the time for free:

- 'Big Ben' [J2 77] or St Stephen's Tower at the Houses of

Parliament. Visible from north, south, east and west, 'Big Ben' can also be heard on BBC Radio 4 as it strikes on the hour. This is considered to be the 'Walker's Clock' since its chimes are derived from the aria in Handel's *Messiah*, one line of which is, 'And by Thy Power no foot shall slide'.

- Fortnum & Mason on Piccadilly, W1 [G1 77].
- Selfridges. Above the main entrance on the south face of the department store facing Oxford Street [D6 60].
- Piccadilly Circus. The LED display to the north of the circus.
- St Thomas's Hospital [K2 77]. A roadside advertising hoarding to the south of the building near the down-ramp leading to the Florence Nightingale museum.
- Paddington Station [B6 60]. Inside the station, on platform 1.
- Bar Italia. Note that this clock is correct twice a day only.
- Oxford Street. Ornamental signpost to Gee's Court [E6 60] and St Christopher's Place.
- Hampton Court. Astrological clock on the inner front of Anne Boleyn's Gateway.
- King's Cross and St Pancras stations [J3 61].
- White Cube² [E3 62]. As a by-product of Jay Joplin's cultural annexation of east London, we now have a digital public clock on the south side of Hoxton Square.

HALF-FINISHED PUBLIC CHRONOMETRIC DEVICES Once for the benefit of seafarers, the red ball which sits atop of the Greenwich Observatory drops at noon, GMT. (Note: this means that the ball drops at 1.00 during British Summer Time.)

At one time, 'a beautiful and useful application for the

telegraph' was planned when the falling of the red ball was to send an electrical charge to a similar ball on the telegraph office near Charing Cross, carrying the time to central London.

SUNDIALS The Horniman Museum [HI 111] (London Road, Forest Hill, SE23) has the following sundials:

- direct west-facing vertical sundial
- 'scaphe' or bowl sundial
- stained-glass vertical dial
- analemmatic sundial
- ceiling dial in the Centre for Understanding the Environment
- 'butterfly' horizontal dial
- Horniman horizontal dial
- Horniman Logo Double Polar Dial.[56]

Walkers who wish to emulate Mr Charles Dickens and loiter in the Earlham Street area in the west of Covent Garden will notice the Seven Dials [J6 61], a monument to Mr Neal, famous for his aromatherapy and dairy and street-naming enterprises, at the junction of Earlham, Monmouth, and Mercer Streets and Short's Gardens.

fitness

Walking is good for you. In a recent survey, it was found that walking breaks down dangerous fats and that just 20 minutes of walking per day can improve your fitness. Although it is better to walk than to sit all day, there is no increase in fitness when walking for longer periods of time.

Another recent study has shown however that walking, being a 'nonvigorous activity, is confirmed to have beneficial effects on insulin sensitivity, the potential for prevention of related chronic diseases, including non-insulin-dependent diabetes mellitus and cardiovascular disease, may be considerable because interventions could be designed that incorporate an already common and presumably acceptable behaviour [walking] that is inexpensive and accessible to large segments of the population.' (Elizabeth Mayer-Davis, PhD, from the University of South Carolina-Columbia.[57])

BREATHING Breath deeply. In through the nostrils, out through the mouth. Inhale oxygen. Exhale carbon dioxide. The human body is a simple machine on this level. Nothing much distinguishes it from other mammals that roam the planet but the human species has a habit of wishing it were different, something more. It has extended itself into realms where it physically should not be – it has built spacecraft, but all the while it has a desire to influence even greater things. Rather than exhale only carbon dioxide, it wants to exhale carbon monoxide. Rather than excrete only small amounts of fecal matter from one orifice, it desires to cover the whole world with shit, beyond even the 'dirty-protests' into the shittiest of shit fests imaginable. It has built machines to fulfil these desires; one such is the internal combustion engine, another is sales and marketing.

Walking in London, you will be acutely aware of these machines and how they operate on you and the environment.

pollutants

You will shift around 20 litres of air per minute when walking. If that air is polluted, your body can suffer as a consequence. The UK government's Department of the Environment, Transport and the Regions has this to say about the way some pollutants can damage your health.[58]

> Nitrogen dioxide, sulphur dioxide and ozone: these gases irritate the airways of the lungs, increasing the symptoms of those suffering from lung diseases.
> Particles: fine particles can be carried deep into the lungs where they can cause inflammation and a worsening of the condition of people with heart and lung diseases.
> Carbon monoxide: this gas prevents the normal transport of oxygen by the blood. This can lead to a significant reduction in the supply of oxygen to the heart, particularly in people suffering from heart disease.

how to avoid intake of pollutants

USE SIDE STREETS Remember that London's roads form a grid-like pattern, running mostly on north–south or east–west axes. This forms an archipelago of street-clusters; regular, quiet ground for you to walk on. If your route follows a main arterial roadway, try to walk on parallel, secondary streets. You will only meet main roads to cross them and will be free from the densities of pollution that can cause you problems.

WEAR A MASK This is fine as long as it's the correct kind of mask. Cyclists have been wearing masks for years now, but some find that the heavy breathing induced both by their physical exertion and the extra effort needed to draw air through the filter can result in more pollutants entering the wearer's lungs.

Many prefer the 'surgeon's' type of mask which hooks over the ears and has the advantage over other forms of face mask in that it turns the tables, making the wearer appear to be the exhaler of some rare and virulent disease.

Novelty cartoon-character masks cannot be recommended in any circumstance. White-collar bank robbery has made such accessories obsolete.

CHECK AIR-POLLUTION STATISTICS On some summer days, when the sun has been shining for what seems like months on end and the cool calming easterly winds have headed south for their vacation, there'll be no need for you to check the papers for the official stats. Your lungs will tell you when the emissions are exceeding legal levels. However, the National Air Quality Information Archive provides accurate, hourly readings of many types of pollutant from more than 20 sites across metropolitan London.[59]

Air pollution statistics as walk generator
Use statistics to your advantage through the application of the following techniques:

1 Choose to walk in areas that report lowest (or highest) air pollution statistics.

2 Abstract the data in the National Air Quality Information Archive online service and use it to generate data for other variables. For example, the following table shows carbon monoxide data for one month:

0.50	0.50	0.70	0.90	1.20	1.00
0.70	0.90	1.10	0.60	0.40	1.30
1.10	0.80	0.60	0.60	1.00	1.00
1.30	0.90	0.90	1.00	1.00	1.00
1.30	0.87	1.20	1.30	0.40	1.10

The data contained in this table could be transposed in many ways, for example, into percentages of minutes (0.50 = 30 seconds; 1.30 = 83 seconds) or hours and minutes (0.50 = 50 minutes; 1.30 = 90 minutes). Use this data to determine how long you will walk. The data could also generate directional information, for example, 0.50 = 50 degrees; 1.30 = 130 degrees.

illness

Even when you are healthy, it is possible to use illness to give structure or to generate walks. Epidemics give you good cause to walk, if only to get away from them. In this situation, walking is determined by rumour, gossip and statistics referring to the number of those ill and their location. Areas where the disease is most virulent will act to repel the walker, forcing them back in search of less-infected districts.

An early example of a walk given structure in this way this can be found in *A Journal of the Plague Year* by Daniel Defoe. Written in 1722, it chronicles, among other things, the journey of three men fleeing from the plague as it took a grip on London. They are a soldier/biscuit maker, sailor/sail maker and a joiner who become increasingly concerned that the Black Death is making its way towards them in Wapping. Several times their way is blocked by constables who, along with the watchmen, enforce the laws of internment, imposed to restrict the flow of pedestrian disease-carriers.

WALK TO ESCAPE THE PLAGUE

Start in Wapping, east to Ratcliff Highway, as far as Ratcliff Cross. Head north, leaving Stepney church on your left. Carry on to Poplar, Bromley, Bow. Turn back at Bow Bridge. Head for Old Ford and Homerton, 'the long divided town of Hackney', the Great North Road to Stamford Hill and then east across the River Lea to Walthamstow, Epping, Woodford and end up in Waltham.

Techniques for escaping the city in times of plague
Travel north with the sun on your back, not in your eyes.
Walk into the wind and away from infected areas.
Take a tent.
Take a hatchet and mallet to build a shelter.
Take a horse.
Take a gun.
Stay away from itinerant salesmen.

injury

ANKLE INJURY If you suspect that you have damaged your ankle ligaments in any way, follow the 'RICE' procedure:

Rest. Stop walking
Ice. Wrap some ice in a towel. Place it on the ankle in a cycle of '20-minutes on, 40-minutes-off'.
Compression. Not too tight!
Elevation. Put your feet up.
(Then get professional medical advice.)[60]

SHIN SPLINTS A burning sensation down the front of the shins, experienced when beginning your walk or when accelerating is commonly known as 'shin splints'. A remedy is suggested by Mark Fenton at walkingmag.com:

> Up: Stand up on your tiptoes.
> Side: Roll your feet so that you're standing on their outside edges.
> Back: Lift your toes as high as possible, so you're standing back on your heels.
> Down: Rest both feet flat on the ground.
> Repeat for 10 cycles.[61]

PREVENTION OF INJURY Walking on pavements will increase the stress on the ankle joints and connective tissue. Some simple preventative measures can be taken:

1 Wear the correct shoes for the job. Don't wear running or climbing shoes when walking.
2 Don't wear damaged shoes. Judged on physical condition alone, walking shoes only last for 500 miles or six months on average. If your shoes are worn, this is the excuse you've been waiting for. Purchase some new ones immediately.
3 Hippies of any persuasion, don't walk barefoot on pavements. This is not northern California. London's streets threaten to upset your karma with everything from chewing-gum to broken glass and dog shit. Walk with care.

BLISTERS Blister prevention is best achieved though wearing appropriate footwear, socks and taking regular breaks from walking. London's extensive network of cafés will prove a great help in this regard.

Make sure that insoles don't stick to the soles of the feet. Any undue sticking will lead to blistering. Confounding popular belief, it has been shown that cotton socks lead to twice as many blisters as acrylic socks. Acrylic fibre is made in layers that allow movement between the inside of the shoe and the foot, movement that would otherwise be performed by the skin of the foot.

If you need treatment, from lancing to more *laissez-faire* approaches, you could do worse than consult 'mother nature.com'.[62]

SHOES FOR DIABETICS Since some diabetics may lose the feeling in their feet, any trauma suffered such as blisters or ulcers may pass undetected. It is therefore imperative that protective footwear is worn. Medicool Inc.'s 'Urban Walkers' 'ensure proper biomechanical support' to 'reduce shear force and provide maximum comfort'.[63]

blood

You may find spots of dark red blood at your feet. This is most commonly found when walking on Saturday, Sunday or Monday mornings, the result of a weekend of pub and /or street fighting.

The chalky surface of contemporary pavements takes the lustre off most spillage over time, but watch for different qualities in cobblestone or tile. Dark Tarmac, having an open surface when new that wicks away liquid, disguises most bodily fluid.

It is very often difficult to ascertain which spots were spilled first. Trails often consist of similarly sized globs of blood scattered at regular intervals with no apparent increase or decrease in flow. But look for discarded tissues or blood-soaked clothing as indications of the site of the causal incident.

> Device: to structure short and often dangerous walks, you can follow the spots of blood to their point of origination or termination.

clothing

Walk in comfort. Ask any fan of the great Che Guevara about the worst aspect of the hard-fought guerilla war against Batista and they will tell you it was the stench of the bearded one's feet brought on by the foot disease mazamorra. Thanks to Che, we now know that the first consideration of any urban warrior is footwear.

In recent years the humble trainer has risen to dizzy heights; once only fit for the likes of Sirs Jimmy Saville and Cliff Richard we now all own, have owned or know someone who owns a pair.

Innovations in arch-support technology have increased the enjoyment factor while lessening the strain of lateral torsion on the medial ligaments. But besides this, it's the look and the feel of your footwear that is most worthy of consideration here.

looking good

To the question, 'How do I look?' should come the reply 'Very good'. In other circumstances, anything else would result in feelings of frustration and inadequacy. In our situation, priming ourselves to walk London, it could also result in ridicule and physical harm.

TRAINERS Consider the merits of each brand carefully:
- Nike. Solidly middle-class wear in the UK. Makes for

Merell

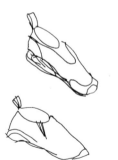

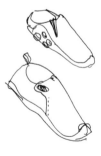

safe walking in Richmond, Chiswick and Soho (Airmax only) but can spell danger elsewhere.

- Airwalk. Skaters are not pedestrians.
- Vans. Likewise.
- Reebok. Cheap, white and British confers immediate 'from hereness' on wearer. Classics only please. Ladies wear 1999 'birth stone' series; early months in particular demand.
- Adidas. You can flirt with the old school, but only if you remember Keegan first time round. Out of the running, literally.
- Acupuncture. Unless you're Robbie Williams and can afford to buy your way out of any fashion faux pas, forget anything marked with an 'A'. A is the answer to every question except 'what letter do I wear conspicuously on my shoes?'
- Merrell. OK, I'm biased here. They've served me well in the research I've had to do, out there in all weathers.

SHIT ON YOUR SHOES London has an intimate relationship with faecal matter. Its lost rivers were once choked by human waste, the Thames flowing ripe to the shores of Essex and Kent. If, as they say, mud sticks, excrement is even more difficult to shift. Get to know it. Get to respect it. But get it on your shoes and you'll know about it. Here's how to avoid it.

There are three main types of faeces that you'll encounter when walking in London: dog, horse and pigeon, though special mention should also be made of the fox, who makes up for what it lacks in ubiquity in stench alone. The droppings of rat and mouse present no immediate risk to the walker as they are only noticeable indoors. Much of the Spitalfields area, for example, is rat-infested. Evidence of this will be made apparent to the walker on early-morning forays; the bloated sewer-water-sodden corpses littering the backstreets until crushed by the trash chariots of work-shy waste disposal operatives.

Dog: ubiquitous and perennial, the dog poses by far the greatest threat to the walker. Dogs have regular bowel movements. Time of feed and time/duration of 'walkies' will determine these.

Proximity to parkland is the single determining factor when judging the likelihood of there being 'dog do' on the pavement. Seasonal changes apply: in winter, many dog-owners fail to match the earlier closing time of public parks with the demands of their mutts. This can lead to faecal build-up around parks, presenting a danger to the walker where least expected. Light is often good in Autumn, enabling dog-logs to be seen in advance, but falling leaves often obscure the offending material. Beware.

Dog ownership is most popular in time-rich areas, therefore both super-rich and ultra-poor have equal tendencies toward dog ownership.

HOW DO YOU KNOW WHEN YOU'VE STEPPED IN IT? There are four tell-tale signs: you smell it; someone else smells it; leaves gather on shoes; dogs follow you.

Horse: horses are common in some parts of London – Stepney for example – but are most noticeable in the royal districts. Horses in Hyde Park rarely stray from Rotten Row [C2, D2 76] and New Ride, but the evidence of them having been elsewhere is unmistakable. Look for the piles of green

dog   shit

need-a-toilet-walk
or stepped-in-shit-walk

dung and straw in the Mall and Horseguards Parade [H1 77] – you can tell where royalty have been – or anywhere after a football match. Horse shit is something you take a detour round rather than tread in, so it presents little in the way of underfoot hazard.

Pigeon: some consider London's pigeons to be vermin, rats with wings. There are some parts of the town, notably Trafalgar Square [H1 77], where pigeon guano is a real risk.

Most dangerous for the walker is the pavement which runs around the eastern side of the Square, under the trees opposite South Africa House. A shower of of bird lime rains constantly on this area. Avoid.

Leicester Square [H7 61] is a magnet for roosting birds, mainly starlings. Beware when walking beneath the trees at dusk.

Fox: pungent turds with musky overtones indicate that foxes have been on the prowl. They are particularly common around London's markets and railways.

HATS Some types of hat – and the reactions they provoke:

- Kangol flat caps (worn backwards): humour; (worn correctly): consternation
- baseball caps: bemusement, suspicion
- rabbit fur 'Mad Bomber' hats: apprehension
- multi-coloured woven skull cap with sequins: sympathy, anger, violence
- motorcycle helmet: fear, apprehension
- bobble hat with long tassels: knowing references to *Elle* or *Dazed & Confused*.

Warning to hat wearers:
Wearing a hat on the Underground is a risky business; you will be stopped at every turnstile and manual check-point. Whenever your crumpled ticket genuinely triggers that 'seek assistance' angry red glare, you will notice hatless passengers being waved through the barrier with an ease you will come to envy.

feeling good

You're going to walk for miles, saunter for days with the aid of this book, so forget what I've said about looks, it's the feel of your footwear that is of ultimate importance.

FOOTWEAR OVERHAUL One thing you can do in the meantime, if you don't want to buy new shoes for your travels, is to overhaul your present ones.

For very cheap insoles for any size of boot or shoe, make your way to Cheshire Street [F4 63] off Brick Lane, E1, late on a Sunday morning. Here you'll find a stall which not only retails such footwear enhancements but also boasts a stall-holder who doles out sound and useful advice on every purchase. 'Walk in comfort', I was told as I parted with my quid-fifty. As both advice and blessing, I take it with me where ever I go. Do the same.

FOOTBATH A tip from the late Pat Phoenix, *Coronation Street*'s flame-haired soap siren: after a tough day on your feet, soak them in Lenor fabric conditioner. Magic.

SMELL Many London streets have their own particular and persistent smells. Some are pleasant, for example the smell of cakes in St Martin's Street [H7 61] near the National Gallery. Others, such as the back streets running adjacent to

Lower Regent Street and Haymarket [H1 77], stink of stale urine and should be avoided on hot summer days, even when you are tempted to take a short cut.

TOILETS As a rule of thumb, it is better to use the lavatories in shops than the public toilets that either charge an entrance fee or sail close to the twilight zone of public hygiene legislation.

ENTRAPMENT OF TRESPASSERS Like their fellow English countrymen, Londoners tend to be proud of their property. Most are happy for you to make your way alongside their splendid residential and business premises. The very few, however, will trick you into trespass or fool you into thinking you have already trespassed, just for sport.

> Warning: one household in Cleaver Street, Kennington [A5 78], keeps its front door open to the street to allow its bulldog to scent the air and rush towards the passer-by. Once growling and snarling, the householders join in the fracas, bawling at the innocent walker, hurling accusations of dog-baiting. Be warned.
> Another warning: Vinopolis in Bankside [C1 78] usurps the public pavement and diverts it into firing distance of its own private lobby area. While you are not trespassing, you can soon feel as if you are. Remember: no purchase necessary.

paper random-walk generator

This is one way to use this device:

1 Make a note of the street on which you are located.
2 Count the letters in the street name, excepting the words 'street', 'road', 'avenue', etc.
3 Manipulate the device a number of times equal to that of the number of letters in the street name.
4 Open the device. This will expose the directional information to you.
5 Count around the points (N, E, S, W, etc.) a number of times equal to that of the number of letters in the second part of the street name (Street, Road, Avenue, etc.).
6 Fold back the flap to reveal distance information.
7 You now have enough information to walk in one direction for a number of streets or of minutes: you decide.
8 Repeat 1.

square paper

1. fold twice lengthwise
   and unfold again.

2. fold corners
   towards
   the center. →
   (neater than this drawing, please.)

3. and again.

4. turn it round.

   ... and again

   all folds are on the back

5. label this side as shown here:

6. unfold those corners and label

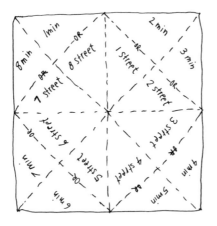

7. Fold back as in step Nr. 5

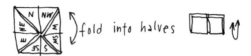 fold into halves

8. move outer corners towards the center

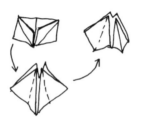

9.

lift corners up

from top

↑ section from side

10.

~~close~~
open and close as
many times as letters
in streetnames to
find desired direction.

walk this way

The following table lists a selection of postcodes for you to walk, set against ways to walk them.

Fill in the blanks using an appropriate system of notation. For example, a simple 'x' or '√' to indicate the possibility of performing each act of walking within the bounds of each postal district; or a figure within the range 0 to 10 to indicate the level of ease or of restriction that you felt as you walked in each area.

Use the table to build up a profile of the city. Compare your table with those of other walkers. Where does your city intersect with theirs? Use the table as a template and add rows and columns where required.

	N1	NW1	EC1	E1	SE1	SW1	W1
accompany							
advance							
amble							
ambulate							
bounce							
creep							
crawl							
canter							
continue							
cover							

	NI	NWI	ECI	EI	SEI	SWI	WI
dance							
dart							
drag							
escort							
flit							
file							
flounce							
follow							
gad							
gambol							
goose-step							
graze							
gander							
go							
haunt							
hike							
hoof							
hurry							
jaunt							
jog							
lead							
limp							
loll							
lurch							
march							
meander							
mince							
move							
pace							
pad							
parade							

london walking

	N1	NW1	EC1	E1	SE1	SW1	W1
patrol							
plod							
prance							
proceed							
promenade							
prowl							
pussyfoot							
range							
reel							
roam							
ramble							
rove							
rush							
sashay							
saunter							
scurry							
shamble							
shuffle							
sidle							
skip							
skidaddle							
slink							
skulk							
slide							
slither							
slog							
sneak							
stagger							
stamp							
stray							
stalk							

	NI	NWI	ECI	EI	SEI	SWI	WI
steal							
step							
stride							
stomp							
stride							
strut							
stroll							
stumble							
swagger							
sweep							
swish							
tail							
tip-toe							
trip							
trot							
tour							
track							
traipse							
tramp							
tread							
trudge							
retrace							
traverse							
trek							
troll							
waltz							
wander							
wobble							
waddle							
wend							
wind							

bridge typology

A typology of bridges, used and disused, across the Thames from the Tower upstream to Hampton Court, excluding the access bridges at Thames Ditton Island and Eel Pie Island.

TOWER BRIDGE

Postcodes: E1 and SE1
Districts: Tower Hill–Bermondsey
Date opened: 1894
Construction: 'steel frame clad in stone'
Number of spans: three
Pedestrian access: yes

LONDON BRIDGE

Postcodes: EC4 and SE1
Districts: Monument–Borough Market
Date opened: 1972
Construction: 'pre-stressed concrete cantilevers'
Number of spans: three
Pedestrian access: yes. At north end: from King William Street; from east and west sides via steps from River Walk footpath. At south end: from Borough High Street; from east side via steps to river footpath and from west via steep flight of steps next to statue of Gryphon that leads towards Southwark Cathedral, Clink Street and Bankside
Song: 'London Bridge is falling down'
View: excellent view into the West End and downriver as far as Canary Wharf. Tower of London visible, as are 'HMS Belfast', Monument and the Lloyds Building. Especially good at night when buildings are lit
Illumination: sides flat-lit by white light from below
Note: for a quiet life, use the

western pavement as it's always the quieter of the two; commuters use the east side to and from London Bridge station

CANNON STREET RAILWAY BRIDGE
Postcodes: EC4 and SE1
Districts: Cannon Street–Southwark
Date opened: 1866
Construction: 'shallow plate girders on cast-iron fluted Doric piers'
Number of spans: five
AKA: Alexandra Bridge
Pedestrian access: no

SOUTHWARK BRIDGE
Postcodes: EC4 and SE1
Districts: Mansion House–Bankside
Date opened: 1921
Construction: 'steel'
Distinguishing features: yellow and green; ornate lamp standards. *Financial Times* building to south
Number of spans: five
Pedestrian access: yes. At north end: incline from Lower Thames Street. From south; from east via steps from river or from rear of FT building's carpark; from west via stone steps on river walk

Note: a quiet bridge. Light traffic use compared to others. Almost silent if you cross late at night. Dimly lit footpath

MILLENNIUM FOOTBRIDGE
Postcodes: EC4 and SE1
Districts: Mansion House–Bankside
Date opened (and closed): 2000
Construction: steel and aluminium
Length: 320 metres
Width: 4 metres
AKA: 'The wobbling bridge'
Pedestrian access: none at time of writing
Webcam: http://www.mbridge.ft.com/blankhi.html#

BLACKFRIARS RAILWAY BRIDGE WEST
Postcodes: EC4 and SE1
Districts: Blackfriars–Southwark
Date opened: 1864; now disused
Construction: 'wrought-iron lattice girder bridge, carried on splendid Romanesque cast-iron columns with massive pylons'
Pedestrian access: no

BLACKFRIARS RAILWAY BRIDGE EAST
Postcodes: EC4 and SE1
Districts: Blackfriars–Southwark

Date opened: 1886
Construction: 'wrought iron faced with cast iron'
AKA: 'St Paul's Bridge'
Number of spans: five
Pedestrian access: no

BLACKFRIARS BRIDGE
Postcodes: EC4 and SE1
Districts: Blackfriars–Southwark
Date opened: 1869
Construction: 'wrought iron faced with cast iron on granite piers'
Distinguishing features: white and red. Circular, floral, gold ornaments. Express Building to south
View: poor to the east (restricted by railway bridge). West towards South Bank and its beaches, at low tide
Number of spans: five
Pedestrian access: yes
Complicated underpass at north side, though provides access to additional sheltered seating at riverside
Other observations: appears narrow and quiet. An intimate bridge compared to London or Waterloo Bridges. Large areas of stone seating on either side of

bridge, positioned over piers, provide shelter from wind and a place to meet

WATERLOO BRIDGE
Postcodes: WC2 and SE1
Districts: Victoria Embankment–Waterloo
Date opened: 1942
Construction: 'cantilevered reinforced-concrete box girders'
Number of spans: five
AKA: The Strand Bridge; Ladies Bridge
Pedestrian access: yes. Footpath from Strand to north, Waterloo Road and the old 'Bullring', now the IMAX Cinema to south. Step access in both north and south: north, from east and west on to Victoria Embankment; from south, step access from next to National Theatre and side of National Film Theatre café

HUNGERFORD RAILWAY BRIDGE
Postcodes: WC2 and SE1
Districts: Victoria Embankment–Waterloo
Date opened: 1864
Construction: 'wrought-iron lattice girder bridge' two brick piers, four

concrete piers
Number of spans: nine
AKA: Charing Cross Bridge
Pedestrian access: yes. North via
east side of Charing Cross
concourse, steps from Villiers
Street, or steps from outside river
entrance to Embankment tube.
South via steps from South Bank
middle, Festival Hall concourse
Note: narrow footpath of Tarmac
on wood. Prone to puddling.
Movement when trains pass. Two
passing/viewing places. Well-used
sticker-zone

WESTMINSTER BRIDGE
Postcodes: SW1 and SE1
Districts: Westminster–Lambeth
Date opened: 1862
Construction: 'cast iron'
Number of spans: seven
Pedestrian access: yes

LAMBETH BRIDGE
Postcodes: SW1 and SE1
Districts: Westminster–Lambeth
Date opened: 1832
Construction: 'steel arch'
Number of spans: five
Pedestrian access: yes

VAUXHALL BRIDGE
Postcodes: SW1 and SE1
Districts: Pimlico–Lambeth
Date opened: 1906
Construction: 'steel arches on
granite piers'
Number of spans: five
AKA: The Regent's Bridge
Pedestrian access: yes

GROSVENOR BRIDGE
Postcodes: SW1 and SW8
Districts: Victoria–Battersea
Date opened: 1866
Construction: steel arches,
wrought-iron piers clad in concrete
Number of spans: five
AKA: Victoria Railway Bridge
Pedestrian access: no

CHELSEA BRIDGE
Postcodes: SW1 and SW8
Districts: Chelsea–Battersea
Date opened: 1934
Construction: suspension bridge
Pedestrian access: yes

ALBERT BRIDGE
Postcodes: SW3 and SW11
Districts: Chelsea–Battersea
Date opened: 1873
Construction: cantilever and

suspension hybrid
Number of spans: three
Pedestrian access: yes

BATTERSEA BRIDGE
Postcodes: w3 and sw11
Districts: Chelsea–Battersea
Date opened: 1890
Construction: cast-iron arches
Number of spans: three
Pedestrian access: yes

BATTERSEA RAILWAY BRIDGE
Postcodes: sw10 and sw11
Districts: Chelsea–Battersea
Date built: 1861
Construction: wrought-iron
Number of spans: five
Note: very similar in appearance to
Southwark Bridge
AKA: West London Extension
Railway Bridge
Pedestrian access: no. Bridge is
enclosed by the Chelsea Harbour
complex on the north bank and is
subject to its strict security

WANDSWORTH BRIDGE
Postcodes: sw6 and sw18
Districts: Fulham–Wandsworth
Date opened: 1940
Construction: 'steel-plate girder

cantilever'
Number of spans: three
Pedestrian access: yes

PUTNEY RAIL BRIDGE
Postcodes: sw6 and sw15
Districts: Fulham–Putney
Date opened: 1889
Construction: lattice-girder
Number of spans: five
Pedestrian access: via Ranelagh
Gardens on the north side. Follow
tunnel on the west side through to
the east and up wide steps; part of
the Thames Path

PUTNEY BRIDGE
Postcodes: sw6 and sw15
Districts: Fulham–Putney
Date opened: 1886
Construction: granite
Number of spans: five
Note: identified by clusters of
orange-capped gaslights
AKA: Fulham Bridge
Pedestrian access: yes. A wide
bridge, difficult to cross its three
lanes of south-bound traffic

HAMMERSMITH BRIDGE
Postcodes: w6 and sw13
Districts: Hammersmith–Barnes

Date opened: 1887
Construction: suspension bridge
Pedestrian access: yes
Illumination: yes. Lights switched
on by the mayor, Councillor
Andrew Slaughter, on 17 March
2000
Note: closed for repair in the late
1990s, the bridge is now open to
traffic again, but with priority
given to buses. Often closed due to
bomb damage[64]

BARNES RAILWAY BRIDGE
Postcodes: W4 and SW13
Districts: Chiswick–Barnes
Date opened: 1895
Construction: 'wrought-iron
bowstring'
Note: is there still a disused bridge
nearby?
Pedestrian access: yes

CHISWICK BRIDGE
Postcodes: W4 and SW14
Districts: Chiswick–Mortlake
Date opened: 1933
Construction: 'concrete arches with
Portland stone facing'
Number of spans: three
Pedestrian access: yes

KEW RAILWAY BRIDGE
Districts: Gunnersbury–Kew
Date opened: 1869
Construction: 'wrought-iron
lattice-girders carried on ornate
cast-iron piers'
Pedestrian access: no. Thames Path
runs beneath the bridge which
carries London Underground
District Line trains

KEW BRIDGE
Districts: Brentford–Kew
Date opened: 1903
Construction: granite
Note: webcam at http://www.
bbc.co.uk/londonlive/traveland
weather/cctv/camdir04021r.html
Pedestrian access: yes

RICHMOND LOCK
Districts: St Margaret's–Richmond
Date opened: 1890
Construction: ornate light green
and cream ironwork. Dual
pathways above lock mechanism
Note: dogs not to off leash or to
foul. No cycling. Melted steps at
both western (second and last
flights) and eastern approaches.
Affords access to Old Deer Park
and its several obelisks

Pedestrian access: yes. Step access to north side only of eastern approach

TWICKENHAM BRIDGE
Districts: St Margaret's–Richmond
Date opened: 1933
Construction: 'three-hinged reinforced concrete arches'; bronze balustrades
Pedestrian access: yes

RICHMOND RAILWAY BRIDGE
Districts: St Margaret's–Richmond
Date opened: 1908
Construction: steel
Pedestrian access: no

RICHMOND BRIDGE
Districts: Twickenham–Richmond
Date opened: 1777
Construction: 'masonry bridge faced with Portland stone'
Number of spans: five
Pedestrian access: yes
Note: oldest surviving Thames crossing in London. Eastern riverside arch is an excellent echo chamber

TEDDINGTON WEIR SUSPENSION BRIDGE
Districts: Twickenham–Richmond
Date opened: 1888
Construction: 'steel towers protected by concrete'
Note: 'cyclists must dismount'
Pedestrian access: yes, via ramp access

KINGSTON RAILWAY BRIDGE
Districts: Hampton Wick–Kingston upon Thames
Date opened: 1907
Construction: steel
Pedestrian access: no. Enclosed by private riverside property, Burgoin Quay, to the west

KINGSTON BRIDGE
Districts: Hampton Wick–Kingston upon Thames
Date opened: 1828
Construction: 'brick faced with stone'
Pedestrian access: yes

HAMPTON COURT BRIDGE
Districts: Hampton Court–East Molesey
Date opened: 1933
Construction: 'reinforced concrete with stone and brickwork facing'
Pedestrian access: yes

site notes

http://www.

1 greenchannel.com/slt/substant.htm
2 geography.about.com/education/geography/library/
  weekly/aa060297.htm
3 ix.net.au/~als/impnav.htm
4 geocities.com/~jdcjr/Songs/DontDillyD.html
5 2.ios.com/~wordup/wilde/dorgrayp.html
6 eig.com/ssus/ssu9610.htm
7 hup.harvard.edu/F99books/reviews/arcades_project_
  R.html
8 wcsu.ctstateu.edu/~mccarney/fva/Jem_Cohen.html
9 pardo.ch/1996/festival96/present/lostfilm.html
10 geography.about.com/education/geography/library/
  weekly/aa060297.htm
11 library.cornell.edu/Reps/DOCS/howard.htm
12 geog.port.ac.uk/geocomp/geo98/89/gc_89.htm
13 howstuffworks.com/cell-phone4.htm
14, 15 pearlies.co.uk/photos.htm
16 bmf.co.uk/briefing/brief03a.html
17 alamofence.com
18 urbanaccessories.net/bollards.html
19 surreycmc.gov.uk/outreach/eline.htm
20 web.cs.city.ac.uk/~louise/omphalos.html
21 unb.ca/web/transpo/mynet/mtu33.htm

22 ramblers.org.uk/factshts/factsh1.html

23 bak.spc.org/kenningtonpark/

24 rudi.herts.ac.uk/ppo/tf/index.html

25 ex.ac.uk/~ajgibson/scotdata/prices/ex/sheep.html

26 topsoc.org/

27 ordsvy.gov.uk/all_lined_up/maps_on_line2.cfm?image
ID=41

28 cockney.co.uk/film.htm

29 jaffebros.com/lee/gulliver/biography/bio_lecky.html

30 abbeymedia.com/Janweb/bishop.htm

31 roads.detr.gov.uk/roadsafety/walk/index.htm

32 user.itl.net/~wordcraf/lexicon.html

33 visionexpress.co.uk

34 worldcollectorsnet.com/cotswoldcollectables/tufty
history.html

35 tufty.com/tuf-ttc.html

36 ourworld.compuserve.com/homepages/traffic_safety/
history1.htm

37 home.clara.net/tmac/paving/pavpage/edging5.htm

38 usroads.com/journals/p/rej/9710/re971001.htm

39 shef.ac.uk/~ccc/groups/vibgroup/abstracts/phd_pim
entel.html

40 met.police.uk/police/mps/2hq/2nh/2nh-se.htm

41 ted.hyperland.net/

42 vl28.dial.pipex.com/chap05.htm#lighting

43 vl28.dial.pipex.com/chap05.htm

44 ordsvy.gov.uk

45 james-smith.co.uk

46 faqs.org/faqs/uk/transport-london/

46 home.clara.net/tmac/paving/index.htm

47 geocities.com/FashionAvenue/3099/index_e.htm

48 cityintl.com/footwear/glossaryE-L.htm

49 wunderground.com/global/stations/03772.htmlweb
   views.co.uk/london/mbridge.ft.com/blankhi.html#
50 vl28.dial.pipex.com/hazard10.htm
51 cimss.ssec.wisc.edu/wxwise/heatisl.html
52 planetrx.com/condition/cond_detail/info/61_
   introduction.html
53 med.monash.edu.au/medicine/mmc/books/foodfacts/
   html/data/data2a.html
54 bbc.co.uk/horizon/longitudetrans.shtml
55 thecore.nus.edu.sg/landow/victorian/history/dora/dora
   19.html
56 sundials.co.uk/~hornimn.htm
57 pslgroup.com/dg/5ef32.html
58 environment.detr.gov.uk/airq/airpoll/4.htm
59 aeat.co.uk/netcen/airqual/welcome.html
60 apma.org/topics/injury.htm
61 walkingmag.com/qa.asp
62 mothernature.com/library/books/dochomerem1/
   blisters.asp
63 medicool.com/diabetes/urban.html
64 hammersmithbridge.co.uk/

selected bibliography

Allen, Richard, *The Moving Pageant*, Routledge, London and New York (uncorrected proof) 1998

Amis, Martin, *London Fields*, Jonathan Cape, London 1989

Ash, Maurice, *A Guide to the Structure of London*, Adams & Dart, Bath 1972

Bachelard, Gaston, *The Poetics of Space*, Beacon Press, Boston MA 1994 edition

Berkeley, Roy, *A Spy's London*, Leo Cooper, London 1994

Bolitho & Peel, *Without the City Wall*, John Murray, London 1952

BR1938 Naval Ratings' Handbook, Naval Training Department, London 1958

Calle, Sophie, *Double Game*, Violette Editions, London 1999

Calvino, Italo, *Invisible Cities*, Picador, London 1979 edition

de Certeau, Michel, *The Practice of Everyday Life*, University of California Press, Berkeley, Los Angeles and London 1988

Coomer, Martin, *Art London*, Ellipsis London, London, 1999

Corporate Watch & Reclaim the Streets, *Squaring Up to the Square Mile*, J18 Publications (UK) 1999

Defoe, Daniel, *A Journal of the Plague Year*, Penguin, London 1966 edition

Dickens, Charles, *Great Expectations*, Penguin, London 1981 edition

Drummond, Bill, *45*, Little, Brown and Company, London, 2000

Dunn, Nell, *Up the Junction*, Pan Books, London 1966

Dwyer, Nancy, *FluxAttitudes: Heckling catalogue*, Imshoot Uitgevers, Gent 1991

Explorer 161, London South, Ordnance Survey, 1999

Explorer 173, London North, Ordnance Survey, 1999

Fuller, Matthew, 'I am the Mayor of London', *Mute 15*, Skyscraper Digital Publishing, 2000

Garreau, Joel, *Edge City*, Anchor Books, New York 1991

Geographers A–Z Map Co., *A–Z Mini London*, Sevenoaks 1995

Hampton Court Palace, Pitkins Pictorials, London 1971

Hewison, Robert, *Future Tense,* Methuen, London 1990

Home, Stewart, *Red London*, AK Press, London 1994

Hylton, William H (ed.), *Build It Better Yourself*, Rodale Press, Emmaus PA, 1977

Jukes, Peter, *A Shout in the Street,* Faber & Faber, London and Boston MA 1990

MacInnes, Colin, *Absolute Beginners*, Allison & Busby, London and New York 1980 edition

City of Spades, Allison Busby, London and New York 1980

England, Half English, Penguin, London 1966

Mr Love and Justice, Allison & Busby, London and New York 1980

Matthews and Brochie (eds), *Oulipo Compendium*, Atlas Press, London 1998

Melling, John Kennedy, *Discovering London's Guilds & Liveries*, Shire Publications, Princes Risborough 1995

Pope, Simon, 'This is London', *Mute* 10, Skyscraper Digital
    Publishing, 2000
Routh, Jonathan, *Routh's Weekend Guide*, Anthony Blond,
    London 1969
Sinclair, Iain, *Dark Lanthorns*, Goldmark, Uppingham
    1999
    Lights out for the Territory, Granta, London 1997
    Radon Daughters, Jonathan Cape, London 1994
    White Chappell Scarlet Tracings, Granta, London 1998
Trench and Hillman, *London Under London*, John
    Murray, London 1999 edition
Vague, Tom, *Vague 28: Entrance to Hipp – Historical
    Psychogeographical Report on Notting Hill*, Vague,
    London 1997
Weightman, Gavin, *Bright Lights Big City*, Collins &
    Brown, London 1992
Wienreb and Hibbert (eds), *The London Encyclopedia*,
    Macmillan, London 1995 edition